MW00488976

SECOND EDITION

STEP FORWARD

STANDARDS-BASED LANGUAGE LEARNING FOR WORK AND ACADEMIC READINESS

SERIES DIRECTOR
Jayme Adelson-Goldstein

Workbook

OXFORD
UNIVERSITY PRESS

Lise Wanage

OXFORD
UNIVERSITY PRESS

198 Madison Avenue
New York, NY 10016 USA

Great Clarendon Street, Oxford, OX2 6DP, United Kingdom

Oxford University Press is a department of the University of Oxford.
It furthers the University's objective of excellence in research, scholarship,
and education by publishing worldwide. Oxford is a registered trade
mark of Oxford University Press in the UK and in certain other countries

ISBN: 978 0 19 449338 3 (WORKBOOK LEVEL 4)

Printed in China

This book is printed on paper from certified and well-managed sources

ACKNOWLEDGMENTS

Illustrations by: Shawn Banner: 13, 22, 23, 43, 55, 56, 67; John Batten: 9, 41, 70,
83; Kathy Baxendale: 51, 71, 74; Annie Bissett: 29, 46, 72. 85; Kevin Brown/
Top Dog Studios: 24, 49, 57, 74, 81; Bill Dickson/Contact Jupiter: 19, 31, 34;
Jon Keegan: 10, 16, 45, 78; Uldis Klavins: 16, 30; Rose Lowry: 6, 22, 37, 65.

*The publishers would like to thank the following for their kind permission to reproduce
photographs*: Cover, Click Bestsellers/Shutterstock.com; pg. 2 Glowimages/Getty
Images, SelectStock/Getty Images; pg. 3 Minerva Studio/Shutterstock; pg. 4
Ramin Talaie/Contributor/Getty Images; pg. 7 wavebreakmedia/Shutterstock;
pg. 11 Chris Cheadle/Getty Images; pg. 14 Arterra Picture Library/Alamy Stock
Photo; pg. 21 Stuart Dee/Getty Images; pg. 28 Nano Calvo/Alamy Stock Photo;
pg. 29 Art Directors & TRIP/Alamy Stock Photo, Paul Barton/Getty Images; pg.
32 Barry Winiker/Getty Images; pg. 35 Monkey Business Images/Shutterstock;
pg. 39 londoneye/Getty Images; pg. 42 Peopleimages/Getty Images; pg. 44
Ariel Skelley/Getty Images; pg. 53 Michael Schmitt/Getty Images; pg. 55
ESB Professional/Shutterstock; pg. 59 ColorBlind Images/Getty Images; pg. 60
Gavin Rodgers/Alamy Stock Photo, ImagesBazaar/Getty Images; pg. 63
bluestocking/Getty Images; pg. 76 damircudic/Getty Images; pg. 79 Strauss/
Curtis/Getty Images, MBI/Alamy Stock Photo; pg. 84 asiseeit/Getty Images.

CONTENTS

It Takes All Kinds!

A Write the adjectives that describe Genaro and Isabel. Use the words in the box.

~~adventurous~~	artistic	mathematical	social
verbal	quiet	athletic	musical

Genaro...

Isabel...

1. goes rock climbing. _adventurous_

2. exercises at the gym. _____

3. enjoys science and numbers. _____

4. likes parties. _____

5. draws and paints. _____

6. doesn't like noisy places. _____

7. plays the guitar. _____

8. likes to tell stories. _____

B Complete the sentences. Use the words in the box.

an auditory	a visual	a kinesthetic

1. Soo likes to read and study from her class notes.

   She is _____ learner.

2. Jose listens well in class, but he doesn't take a lot of notes.

   He is _____ learner.

3. Maria learns by doing things and using her hands.

   She is _____ learner.

A **Complete the paragraph. Use the sentences in the box.**

> On weekends, I play soccer and exercise.   I don't like to read auto manuals.
> At home, I don't watch TV very often.   I like to do activities with other students.
> ~~I'm an auto mechanic.~~

My Learning Style

I'm a kinesthetic learner. I learn best when I do things and work with my hands. <u>I'm an auto mechanic.</u>
1
I learn more about a car if I work with it.

_____ At school, I would
2
rather practice than listen to a long explanation.

_____ I don't learn very
3
well from sitting in class.

_____ I spend more time fixing things and doing yard
4
work. _____ I'd rather be outside than inside. My goal is to
5
teach new auto mechanics some day, so I can help other kinesthetic learners.

B **Correct the paragraph. Add capital letters and periods.**

        I
        ⱦf you know your learning style, you will be a better learner ⊙ my friend pietro
is a visual learner when we are studying new words in class, pietro always asks
the teacher to write them on the board he has to see the word before he can
say it he also draws a lot of pictures in his vocabulary notebook he says that the
pictures help him remember the new words

C **Look at B. Then rewrite the paragraph.**

   <u>If you know your learning style, you will be a better learner.</u>

   _____

   _____

   _____

   _____

   _____

A Complete the sentences with the simple present. Use the verbs in parentheses.

1. When Mai wants to learn something, she usually ____reads____ a book. (read)

2. When you _____ Luz something, she usually remembers it. (tell)

3. Roberto _____ around the class because he can't sit still. (move)

4. Alonzo forgets new vocabulary if he _____ the words aloud. (not say)

B Complete the sentences with the present continuous. Use the verbs in parentheses.

1. The students ____are preparing____ their final class project. (prepare)

2. Alonzo and Ricardo _____ a play that they wrote. (practice)

3. Luz _____ Mai about her life. (interview)

4. Roberto _____ with a partner. (not work)

5. He _____ photographs. (take)

C Complete the paragraphs with the simple present or the present continuous. Use the verbs in parentheses.

It's 3:30 in the afternoon at a public school in New York, and the teenagers in this picture _____are practicing_____
₁
(practice) their favorite "sport." Yes, these teens are on a team, but not in the usual way. At this moment, they _____ (play)
₂
chess, not basketball.

Chess in the Schools is an organization that works in public schools in cities. It
_____ (teach) one chess
₃
class each week for 16 weeks. Then some students _____
₄
(play) chess in a chess club after school two or three times a week. In the club, students _____ (learn) from each other. One student
₅
says, "Right now, I _____ (work) hard, so I can play with
₆
students from other schools next year."

D **Mark the verbs A (action verb) or S (stative verb).**

A 1. walk   ____ 5. know

____ 2. believe   ____ 6. write

____ 3. paint   ____ 7. ride

____ 4. remember   ____ 8. work

E **Choose the correct verb. Circle *a* or *b*.**

1. Hey! You ____ a mistake.

    a. make   (b.) are making

2. I ____ what you mean.

    a. don't know   b. 'm not knowing

3. We ____ question 2 now.

    a. 're doing   b. do

4. Oh, I ____ what you're saying.

    a. am understanding   b. understand

F **Study the Grammar note. Then circle the correct words in the conversations.**

> **Grammar note: *Look/see* and *listen/hear***
>
> | **Action verbs** | **Stative verbs** |
> |---|---|
> | *look* | *see* |
> | *listen* | *hear* |
>
> *Look/see* and *listen/hear* are pairs of action and stative verbs. The words have similar meanings, but *look* and *listen* are more active. When you want someone to pay attention to something, you say, "Look!" or "Listen!"

1. **A:** Look! Up there! Do you ((see) / look) that?

    B: See what? I'm (looking / seeing), but I don't see anything.

2. **A:** (Listen / Hear) for a moment! Do you (listen / hear) that?

    B: I'm (listening / hearing), but I don't (listen / hear) anything.

3. **A:** I can (see / look) it now. (See / Look)! Over there in the sky.

    B: I'm (seeing / looking)! Oh, I (see / look) it now. It's an airplane.

A **Number the sentences of the conversation in the correct order.**

_____ **Liang:** Well, yes, you have a point. I get nervous because the pronunciation is difficult.

__1__ **Satish:** You know, Liang, I think this class is too easy for you. Don't you agree?

__6__ **Liang:** Thanks, Satish. Maybe you're right. If I practice with you first, maybe it will help.

_____ **Satish:** Oh, come on! You can speak very well. You're just shy and a little nervous.

_____ **Liang:** No, it's not that easy. I understand the grammar, but I can't speak very well.

_____ **Satish:** Yeah, pronunciation is hard. Hey, let's practice together.

B **Match the questions with the answers.**

__b__ 1. Do you feel nervous in class?

_____ 2. Do you like conversation or dislike it?

_____ 3. What does *shy* mean?

_____ 4. Does he usually ask questions?

_____ 5. Does Liang think the pronunciation is easy or difficult?

a. No, he doesn't.

b. No, I don't.

c. He thinks it's difficult.

d. I like it, but I feel shy.

e. It means to be nervous with other people.

C **Look at the conversation in A. Write a new ending.**

Liang: <u>Thanks, Satish. Maybe you're right. If I practice with you first, maybe it will help.</u>

Satish: <u>Practicing together will help me too.</u>

Liang: _____

Satish: _____

Liang: _____

Satish: _____

DO THE MATH Go to page 86.

A Read the article. What are three ways to improve memory?

Unlock Your Memory

Use your body to build memory. Some people say that people remember 90 percent of what they do, 75 percent of what they see, and 20 percent of what they hear. Learning actively can use your whole body. You can stand up and talk aloud as you study, and use your arms, legs, eyes, ears, and voice. This puts more energy into your study time and makes it less boring.

   Relax. Have you ever been unable to remember information on a test but an hour later remembered the information perfectly? This may mean that you were not relaxed during the test. Relaxation allows more blood to go to the brain and lets us think more clearly. Our brains are more awake when we are relaxed, and this helps us to perform better.

   Use visualization. The more visual you can make the learning process, the easier it will be to remember the information. Create mental pictures that you can connect with the information you are trying to learn.

   Now it's your turn to try it! Move your body, relax, and use visualization. See how your memory improves.

B Look at A. Circle *a* or *b*.

1. Some people say that ＿＿ helps you remember more than seeing something.
   a. doing something
   b. hearing something

2. To put energy into your study time, the article suggests ＿＿.
   a. sitting in a quiet place to study
   b. moving around more

3. Relaxation helps us learn because ＿＿.
   a. the brain gets more blood
   b. we get more sleep

4. When you aren't relaxed, you ＿＿.
   a. can't remember information
   b. can think more clearly

5. To visualize something means ＿＿.
   a. to draw a picture on paper
   b. to picture something in your mind

A Look at the quiz. Read the questions. Then check (✓) your answers.

Learning Styles Quiz	Yes 5 points	No 1 point	Sometimes 3 points
1. Do you understand better when you see a picture?			
2. Do you turn on the radio to listen to the news?			
3. Do you like dancing and playing sports?			
4. Can you easily understand maps?			
5. Do you play with things on your desk when you study?			
6. Do you remember spoken directions very easily?			
7. Do you like to eat snacks during a study period?			
8. Do you think movies are more interesting than books?			
9. Do you learn to spell by repeating the letters aloud?			

B Write your points for each question in the chart below. Add the points in each column. The column with the most points is your best learning style. Complete the sentence.

Number	VISUAL	Number	AUDITORY	Number	KINESTHETIC
1		2		3	
4		6		5	
8		9		7	
TOTAL:		TOTAL:		TOTAL:	

I am a/an _____ learner!

LESSON 1 VOCABULARY

A Match the newspaper headlines with the part of the news website.

_b_ 1. Old Town Street Festival Crowded   a. Ad

____ 2. Baseball's Dream Team Wins Again   b. Local News

____ 3. For Sale: 2014 Toyota Pickup Red   c. Sports

____ 4. Letters to the Editor   d. Editorials

____ 5. Young Actress Wins Award   e. Entertainment

____ 6. Best Food for Your Dog! Save 20%   f. Classified Ads

B Complete the paragraph. Use the words in the box.

| top story | traffic report | ~~current events~~ | headlines | weather forecast |

Good evening. I'm David Lorning at Channel 14 in Langston. Stay tuned to Channel 14 for all of the latest news on the _____current events_____ of the day. On the
1
local news tonight, this is the _____:
2
Volunteers in Langston are sending food and tents to the Southeast after last week's terrible hurricane. Then our reporters, Tony Bright and Sue Marshall, will report on the rest of today's _____: a
3
woman rescued from a local river and a robbery at a Langston bank. We all want to know when this rain is going to end, so our own Bill Jones will give this week's

_____. Then John Nolan will give us information about conditions
4
on the roads in his _____.
5

A **Number the sentences of the story in the correct order.**

The Robbery That Wasn't!

_____ The robber looked at her in surprise and said, "Oh, OK."

__1__ A masked man walked into the Trust Bank in Watford yesterday.

__7__ The police searched the neighborhood, but they didn't find the robber.

_____ Ms. Martin looked at the robber and said, "No!"

_____ He then turned and ran out of the bank without the money.

_____ After the robber left, bank employees called the police.

_____ He gave the teller, Louise Martin, a bag and told her to fill it with cash.

B **Look at A. Write answers to the questions. Use complete sentences.**

1. What did the robber want? He wanted money.

2. What did the teller say? _____

3. What did employees do? _____

4. Did the police find the robber? _____

C **Look at the story in A. Write a new ending.**

      The police searched the neighborhood, but they didn't

find the robber. Two hours later, the police received another

call...

_____

_____

_____

_____

_____

_____

_____

A Complete the news story with the past passive. Use the verbs in parentheses.

Red Canyon Fire Under Control

Five homes _____were destroyed_____
                        1
(destroy) by a fast-moving fire in the Red
Canyon area yesterday. Some people said
the fire _____ (start)
                    2
by campers in the area, but firefighters
believe the cause was lightning. Residents
_____ (tell) to leave
              3
the area Monday afternoon. No residents
_____ (injure). However, two firefighters _____
              4   5
(rescue) by team members following an accident. They _____ (take)
                                                              6
by helicopter to Southside Hospital. Firefighters were finally able to control the fire by late
afternoon yesterday.

B Look at A. Circle *a* or *b*.

1. How was the Red Canyon fire started? (a.) by lightning   b. by campers

2. How were the firefighters rescued?   a. by team members   b. by campers

3. How were firefighters taken out?   a. by ambulance   b. by helicopter

4. How was the fire controlled?   a. by a rain storm   b. by firefighters

C Write sentences with the past passive. Use a phrase with *by* + noun.

1. many homes / save / firefighters' quick response
   Many homes were saved by the firefighters' quick response.

2. other fires / start / campers in the area
   _____

3 two firefighters / injure / falling trees
   _____

4. team members / contact / cell phone
   _____

D Write *yes/no* questions. Use the past passive and the words in parentheses.

1. <u>Was the new hospital finished</u>   ? (the new hospital, finish)

2. _____? (the funding for the library, approve)

3. _____? (old train station, damage)

4. _____? (the old train cars, replace)

E Complete the questions.

1. **A:** When <u>was the new school completed</u>   ?

   B: The new school was completed in August.

2. **A:** When _____?

   B: Construction on the new station was finished in September.

3. **A:** Where _____?

   B: The new station was built across the street from the old one.

4. **A:** Why _____?

   B: The old station was replaced because it was too small.

F Study the Grammar note. Then rewrite the sentences with active verbs.

> **Grammar note: Passive vs. active**
>
> | **Passive** | **Active** |
> |---|---|
> | The road was reopened by **the police**. | **The police** reopened the road. |
>
> Writers in English should use active verbs as much as possible.

1. Their house was damaged by the flood.

   <u>The flood damaged their house.</u>

2. The new library was designed by Louisa Wright.

   _____

3. The airport improvements were approved by the city council.

   _____

4. The Red Canyon news story was written by Jeff Young.

   _____

A **Complete the conversation. Use the sentences in the box.**

> Maybe they can put the courts over there, far away from the building.
>
> Well, you know, teenagers need to keep themselves busy.
>
> ~~No, what's it about?~~
>
> I think I'll talk to the committee about it.
>
> No, basketball.

Ray: Hey, did you see this notice written by our building association?

Jose: <u>No, what's it about?</u>

1

Ray: It says that they're building a new recreation center with basketball courts next to our apartment complex.

Jose: Did you say baseball?

Ray: _____

2

Jose: Oh, no. That's going to be too noisy. Kids will play there every night.

Ray: _____

3

Jose: I can understand that, but the people here want to live in a quiet place.

Ray: _____

4

Jose: That's a good idea. _____

5

B **Complete the sentences. Use reflexive pronouns.**

1. They know that teenagers need to keep <u>themselves</u> busy.

2. Mr. Sato went to the meeting by _____.

3. He offered to write the report, but Ms. Moya said, "I'll write it _____."

4. We enjoyed _____ when we watched the game.

A Read the article. How has the *New York Times* stayed the same over the years?

The *New York Times*: An American Tradition

The *New York Times* is one of the leading news sources in the world today. The first issue was published on September 18, 1851, by Henry Jarvis Raymond and George Jones. Over the years, there have been many changes to the *New York Times* company and products, but one thing has stayed the same: they have published a newspaper every day since that day.

One of the biggest changes to the company was in 1996 when the *New York Times* went online at **www.newyorktimes.com**. This meant people all over the world could read the articles the same day they were published. About ten years after that, the company started their first mobile site. This meant that people could see the paper on their cell phones. Since then, the *New York Times* has also released apps for other devices.

In the past, people bought subscriptions to have the newspaper delivered to their homes every day. Today, many people prefer to read their news online, using devices such as their cell phones or tablets, so the *New York Times* offers online options for subscriptions. They also still offer home delivery of the newspaper, which gives readers access to the articles online too.

Although technology has changed the way people get their news, the *New York Times* has remained a leading news source. Because of that, it is an American tradition.

B Look at A. Mark the sentences *T* (true), *F* (false), or *NI* (no information).

__F__ 1. The first issue of the *New York Times* was published 100 years ago.

_____ 2. They have published a newspaper every day since the first one came out.

_____ 3. In 1996, only people with newspaper subscriptions could read articles online.

_____ 4. The apps they added let people read articles on devices like cell phones.

_____ 5. They don't offer home delivery of the newspaper anymore.

A Read the headline and the sentence. Underline the words and punctuation in the sentence that are not in the headline.

Need help?

News headlines often use a "short" form of writing. For example, they leave out forms of *be* from passive sentences and words like *the* and *a*. They also don't use end punctuation, like periods.

Headline
Town of North River Flooded After Heavy Rains
Sentence
The town of North River was flooded after heavy rains.

B Read the headlines. Then write full sentences using the past passive and *a* or *the*. Be sure to use punctuation.

Local Student Awarded Prize for Science Project

1. A local student was awarded a prize for a science project.

Theft Reported by North River Bank

2. _____

Local Soccer Team Defeated by Watford

3. _____

Highway 80 Closed During Hurricane

4. _____

New Bridge Opened Across North River

5. _____

A Read the problems. Then choose the best advice. Circle *a* or *b*.

1. I have a flat tire.

   (a.) Change it!   b. Send a tow truck.

2. It's dark, and I had a breakdown.

   a. Turn on the hazard lights.   b. Get directions.

3. I want the police to know my car's broken down.

   a. Change it!   b. Raise the hood.

4. I've tried everything. The car won't move!

   a. Get directions.   b. Put out safety triangles and call for help.

5. I can't find Laurel Lane. I think I'm lost.

   a. Turn on the hazard lights.   b. Get directions from someone.

B Complete the sentences. Use the words in the box.

| out of gas | ~~locked out of my car~~ | lost | stuck in traffic |

I'm *locked out of my car*.

1

I'm _____.

2

I'm _____.

3

I'm _____.

4

A Number the sentences of the story in the correct order.

> **What Time Was That?**
>
> _____ I asked her, in Spanish, about my next appointment.
>
> _____ However, I understood *las doce*. That means *twelve o'clock*.
>
> _1_ Do you want to hear a funny language-learning story?
>
> _____ A few years ago, I was learning Spanish.
>
> _7_ On Friday, when I arrived for my appointment,
> the office was closed for lunch.
>
> _____ So, one day I tried to practice with my doctor's receptionist.
>
> _____ She said that it was next Friday at *las dos* (two o'clock).

B Read the story in A. Write a new ending.

On Friday, when I arrived for my appointment, the office was closed for lunch.

I knocked on the door, but nobody answered.

_____

_____

_____

_____

_____

C Rewrite the sentences as quoted speech. Add capital letters and punctuation.

1. i said i have an appointment today at twelve o'clock

   I said, "I have an appointment today at twelve o'clock."

2. the receptionist said i'm sorry your appointment isn't until two o'clock

   _____

3. i said i probably got confused about the time

   _____

4. she said i forgot to give you an appointment card

   _____

A Read the quoted speech. Then circle the correct pronoun in the reported speech.

1. Our friends said, "You need a new car."

Our friends said that ((we) / you) needed a new car.

2. My wife said, "I want a van."

My wife said that (I / she) wanted a van.

3. The salesmen said, "We have a nice van here for only $7,000."

The salesmen said that (they / we) had a nice van for only $7,000.

4. I said, "You have to give us a better price."

I said that (you / they) had to give us a better price.

B Complete the sentences with reported speech.

1. The driver said, "The bus has a flat tire."

The driver said that _the bus had a flat tire_____.

2. Magdalena said, "I am waiting on Cedar Street."

Magdalena said that _____.

3. Kiana said, "I want directions to the college."

Kiana said that _____.

4. The bus driver said, "Maple Street isn't too far away."

The bus driver said that _____.

5. The auto mechanic said, "It's going to take 20 minutes to fix it."

The auto mechanic said that _____.

6. Stan said, "I have to take a different bus."

Stan said that _____.

C Complete the sentences with *said* or *told*.

1. Magdalena _____said_____ she had a ride.

2. The bus driver _____ Kiana how to get to the college.

3. Stan _____ he could take a different bus.

4. The auto mechanic _____ us the bus was easy to fix.

5. The bus driver _____ them Maple Street wasn't far.

D **Read the sentences. Rewrite them as reported speech. Use *told*.**

1. The bus driver talked to the riders. He said, "There's been an accident."

   The bus driver told them (that) there had been an accident.

2. Isabel said to her husband, "I'm late."

   _____

3. Ramon called Sienna. He said, "I'm stuck in traffic."

   _____

4. Rosa said to her friend, "The ambulance is coming."

   _____

E **Study the Grammar note. Then complete the conversation. Use reported speech in the present.**

> **Grammar note: Reported speech in present**
>
> When the reporting verb, *say* or *tell*, is in the present, the time of the verb in reported speech doesn't change.
>
> *Molly: Hi dad. I **want** to come home from camp now.*
> *Dad (to mom): Molly **says** (that) she **wants** to come home from camp now.*

Al: I'm locked out of my car.

Bev: It's Al. He says _(that) he's locked out of his car_____.
                                                                    1

Al: I need my extra keys.

Bev: He says _____.
                                          2

Al: The keys are in the desk.

Bev: He says _____.
                                          3

A Complete the conversation. Use the phrases in the box.

> don't we try it?
> ~~I were you, I'd take Island Road east.~~
> a good idea, ma'am.
> about trying Airport Drive to Highway 24 east?
> bet there won't be much traffic.

Amanda: I want to go to Red Beach, please.

Taxi Driver: Do you know the fastest way to Red Beach?

Amanda: If _I were you, I'd take Island Road east._____ Then go over the bridge.
                                                    1

Taxi Driver: There's usually a lot of traffic on the bridge.

Amanda: How _____
                                                    2

Taxi Driver: That's _____ It's longer that way, but
                                          3

                it might be faster.

Amanda: I _____ It
                                          4

                will only take 20 minutes.

Taxi Driver: OK. Why _____
                                                    5

                Please fasten your seat belt! Better safe than sorry, I always say!

B Read the instructions. Rewrite them as reported speech. Use *said* or *told*.

1. The GPS said, "Go straight." (said)

   _The GPS said to go straight._____

2. The gas station attendant said to me, "Don't take Highway 9." (told)

   _____

3. He said, "Take Route 4 instead." (said)

   _____

4. He said to us, "Drive safely." (told)

   _____

5. My father said, "Don't go that way." (said)

   _____

DO THE MATH Go to page 87.

A Read the article. What can drivers do to stay safe in the rain?

How to Drive Safely in the Rain

Here is some good advice about driving safely in the rain.

Keep a safe distance.
According to the National Safety Council, in normal conditions you should stay three seconds behind the car in front of you on the highway. When it's raining, you should be at least two times that distance away. A car needs much more time (and distance) to stop safely on wet roads.

Slow down.
The best way to avoid an accident during wet road conditions is to slow down. Driving more slowly allows the tires to make contact with the road. Most U.S. roads are higher in the middle, so when you have to drive on a wet road, drive in the middle lane. Sometimes the rain is falling very hard. When you can't see well, you are in danger. You should get off the road and park your car until the rain stops.

This car should slow down.

Avoid flooded areas.
Never try to drive across a road that is flooded by rain. You don't know how much water there really is on the road. A pool of water even one foot deep can carry a car away. Emergency workers often don't understand why drivers take risks[1] with flooded roads.

Remember: Keep your distance, slow down, and avoid flooded roads!

[1] risk: a possibly dangerous action

B Look at A. Circle *a* or *b*.

1. When it's raining, drivers should be at least _____ the car in front of them.

   (a.) six seconds away from   b. one second away from

2. The safest lane on a wet road is usually the _____.

   a. side lane   b. middle lane

3 Drivers should _____ if they can't see the road.

   a. get off the road and park   b. stop in the middle of road

4. Emergency workers think that drivers should _____.

   a. not drive on flooded roads   b. take risks

A Read the scene from a TV program. What type of show do you think it is?

The Friday Night Mystery

Act 1

[Scene: In a darkened bedroom, Natalia is standing by the window holding the curtain back. Alexi is sitting up in bed looking confused.]

Alexi: Natalia, <u>it's 2:30 in the morning</u>. What's the matter? *[He¹ reaches over to turn on the light.]*

Natalia: *[Looking out the window and motioning to Alexi with her hand]* Wait. <u>Don't turn on the light</u>. Something is happening outside. ²

Alexi: *[Gets out of bed and crosses to the window]* What's going on?

Natalia: A car is parked in front of the neighbor's house.

Alexi: <u>The neighbors are on vacation</u>. ³

Natalia: I know. It looks like two men. They're climbing over the fence.

Alexi: *[Reaching for his clothes]* <u>I'm going out there</u>. ⁴

Natalia: No! Don't go out! What if they're dangerous?

Alexi: <u>Then I have to call the police</u>. Where's my cell phone?

Natalia: It's on the night⁵ table. <u>Hurry</u>! They just broke ⁶ a window, and they're going into the house.

Alexi: *[Dialing]* What's the license plate of that car?

Natalia: 267-RTN.

B Look at A. Rewrite the underlined text. Use reported speech with *said* or *told*.

1. Alexi said <u>it was 2:30 in the morning.</u>

2. Natalia told Alexi _____

3. _____

4. _____

5. _____

6. _____

A **Complete the sentences. Use the words in the box**

resource center	~~interest inventory~~	career counselor
training course	financial aid	job listings

1. "You can take an _____interest inventory_____ to find a job you'll like."

2. "I need advice about my job. Can I meet with the _____?"

3. "I need money for college. How can I apply for _____?"

4. "I'm interested in learning new job skills. I'd like to take a _____."

5. "The new _____ are posted online once a week.

6. "I hear you can learn a lot about different careers in this _____."

B **Match the words with the definitions.**

1. I only have time for a one-time class. I need _____.

   a. an apprenticeship   (b.) a job-skills workshop

2. I need some work experience, so I can get a job. I need _____.

   a. an internship   b. career and technical training

3. I'd like to learn new skills at work for the job I have now. I need _____.

   a. an online course   b. on-the-job training

A Read Joe's notes. Then complete the cover email.

NOTES FOR COVER EMAIL
Position: auto mechanic
Experience: three years at Gary's Garage on Front Street
Training: two years, Valley Vocational College
Available: immediately

From: Joseph Beck <jbeck@wol.us>
To: andy@tysonautocenter.biz
Re: Auto mechanic position

Dear Mr. Tyson:

I'm writing in response to your job listing for the position of _____auto mechanic_____.
                                                                              1

I have attached my resume.

I trained for _____ at _____. I also have
                       2   3

_____ of experience working at _____.
            4   5

I am _____ to start work _____.
              6   7

I look forward to talking with you soon. You can contact me by phone at

_____ or by email at _____.
            8   9

Sincerely,
Joseph Beck
Cell: 317-962-2953

B Look at A. Circle *a* or *b*.

1. Joseph stated the job he was applying for ____.
   a. in the first paragraph   b. in the second paragraph

2. In the second paragraph, Joseph included information about ____.
   a. his email address   b. his training and experience

3. He did not include information about ____.
   a. the job he is applying for   b. his family and friends

A Complete the paragraph. Use the past perfect and the verbs in parentheses.

Mac's Moving Company needed to hire a new truck driver. After the job listing

_____ had been _____ (be) posted for a week, only two applicants called about
                1

the job. The first, Soon Yung, _____ (not work) as a truck driver
                                              2

before, but he _____ (take) a course at a truck driver training
                         3

school. The second applicant was Arlin. He _____ (drive)
                                                         4

trucks for the ABC Moving Company, but he _____ (have) two
                                                            5

accidents on the job. So after the manager _____ (interview) the
                                                         6

two applicants, she decided not to hire either one!

B Combine the sentences. Use the simple past and the past perfect.
The underlined sentence is the event that happened first.

1. Atim received her certificate. <u>She took an online course.</u>

   <u>Atim received her certificate</u> after <u>she had taken an online course</u>.

2. Atim and Malik went to the job fair. <u>They read a flyer about it.</u>

   _____ after _____.

3. <u>They filled out job applications.</u> They were called for interviews.

   After _____.

4. <u>They passed their job interviews.</u> They were both offered jobs.

   After _____.

5. <u>J. Stevens Co. hired 25 new employees.</u> Their new office opened in September.

   _____ before _____.

C Complete the questions.

1. **A:** _Had Omar worked with computers_ before he got the job at the Computer Superstore?

   B: Yes, he had. He worked with computers at a college workshop last fall.

2. **A:** Why _____ before he started the job?

   B: He hadn't taken the training workshop because it cost too much money.

3. **A:** _____ before he got this one?

   B: No, he hadn't. He had never had a job before this one.

4. **A:** Which manager _____ before he arrived for the interview?

   B: He had spoken to a manager named Mr. Lang.

5. **A:** How long _____ before they finally called him?

   B: He'd waited for two weeks before they finally called him.

D Study the Grammar note. Then complete the sentences. Use *already* and the verb in parentheses.

> **Grammar note: *Already* with the past perfect**
>
> The word *already* is often used with the past perfect. It goes between *had* and the past participle.
>
> When I arrived, the interview **had already started**.

1. When I arrived at school today, the class ____had already finished____. (finish)

2. When Claudia called, the manager _____ at the store. (arrive)

3. When Camille got the job, she _____ the cashier's course. (complete)

4. When my partner came in, we _____ all the furniture in the truck. (put)

5. Xavier _____ dinner when Angie got home. (prepare)

DO THE MATH Go to page 88.

A **Complete the conversation. Use the sentences in the box.**

> Thanks, Mr. Ellis. How about Monday?
>
> Yes, that's the one.
>
> ~~Do you mean working in a hotel?~~
>
> I took a management training course at the Jade Hotel.
>
> I'd been a cashier and an assistant manager in two restaurants.

Mr. Ellis: How are you, Ms. Yan? I'll be interviewing you for the position of hotel manager. So, tell me, what experience have you had?

Ju-li: <u>Do you mean working in a hotel?</u>
1

Mr. Ellis: No, any experience.

Ju-li: Before I came to the United States, _____
2
Now I'm working at the Jade Hotel as a manager. I've been there for three years.

Mr. Ellis: How about management training?

Ju-li: _____
3

Mr. Ellis: I've visited the Jade Hotel. Isn't that the beautiful building near J Street?

Ju-li: _____
4

Mr. Ellis: Well, Ju-li, I've read your resume. You have the right skills for the job. When can you start?

Ju-li: _____
5

B **Read the paragaph. Circle the correct verbs.**

Before Ju-li ((moved) / has moved) to the United States, she
1
(has been / had been) a cashier and an assistant manager.
2
Then she (found / had found) a job at the Jade Hotel. She
3
(worked / has worked) there for three years now. Ju-li
4
(has finished / had finished) a management class before Mr. Ellis
5
called her for the interview. Mr. Ellis (had read / has read)
6
Ju-li's resume before they met.

A Read the interview. How did Indaia Santos decide to be a professional musician?

Indaia Santos

Q: **How did you get started as a musician?**

A: I grew up in Brazil. I was a quiet person then. I spent time alone playing my guitar every day. Later, I met a poet who wanted to make his poems into music. By that time, I'd already written several songs and sung in different music groups for fun. So, I wrote music for 12 of his poems and recorded one of them. That song got popular, so I started a band with my husband and friend.

Q: **What did you do before you were a musician?**

A: I worked at a small shop that sold office supplies. The job was okay, but it wasn't what I wanted to do. I set a career goal to find something I would enjoy more. I took an interest inventory and skills assessment. I learned that being a musician would be a good fit for me. I met the poet later that year.

Q: **Where has your band performed?**

A: We've performed at private parties, coffee houses, street fairs, weddings, and restaurants.

Q: **Is it easy for a musician to earn a living this way?**

A: I have two children, so it's not easy. We work on weekends. Slowly, we have built our business, and through hard work and practice, we stay busy. Did you know that some people think we play for free? People pay for jobs and services, but when it comes to artists, it's different. They think we work just for love and that we don't need money! But we do! Our equipment is expensive. We spend time practicing and getting dressed for the evening. So we have to get paid for our music.

B Look at A. Circle *a* or *b*.

1. When she was younger, Indaia _____.

   a. wrote poems

   (b.) practiced the guitar

2. When Indaia met the poet, she had already _____.

   a. written some songs

   b. written music for his poems

3. Indaia started the band _____ one of her song became popular.

   a. after

   b. before

4. Indaia took an interest inventory _____ she decided to become a professional musician.

   a. after

   b. before

A Read the timeline. Then complete the sentences with the past perfect. Use the words in parentheses.

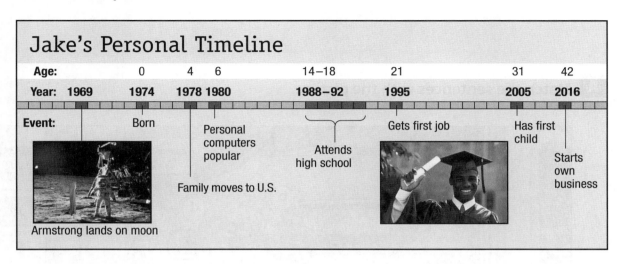

Jake's Personal Timeline

Age:	0	4	6	14–18	21	31	42
Year: 1969	1974	1978	1980	1988–92	1995	2005	2016

Event: Born — Personal computers popular — Family moves to U.S. — Attends high school — Gets first job — Has first child — Starts own business

Armstrong lands on moon

1. When Jake was born, _____ Armstrong had already landed on the moon _____.

   (Armstrong / already / land / on moon)

2. When Jake was four years old, _____.

   (family / just / move / to the U.S.)

3. When his family moved to the U.S., _____.

   (personal computers / not become / popular)

4. When Jake was 15, _____.

   (he / already / start / high school)

5. When Jake got his first job, _____.

   (he / already /graduate / from high school)

6. When he had his first child, _____.

   (he / not / start / his own business)

B Make your own personal timeline. Follow these instructions. Use your own paper.

1. Choose at least four events from your personal life and two or more world events for your timeline.

2. Make a chart for your personal timeline with years, your age, and the events.

3. Write five or six sentences about the timeline. Use the past perfect.

A Match the sentences with the picture.

__d__ 1. She's wearing gloves because the chemicals are corrosive.

_____ 2. There's motor oil on the floor. It's slippery.

_____ 3. He's wearing a mask. Those paint fumes are poisonous.

_____ 4. The customer can't come in here. It's a restricted area.

_____ 5. The office window is broken. It needs to be fixed.

_____ 6. This light has a frayed cord. It needs a new one.

B Circle the correct words.

Parking garages in shopping malls are often ((isolated) / suspicious) areas with
1
very few people around. (Be alert / Be active), especially in the evening. Always
2
stay in areas that are well lit and busy with people. (Avoid / Prevent) walking
3
alone in the parking lot. Have your car keys ready, and keep your eyes open.
Be aware of any suspicious (activities / accidents) around you. If you notice a
4
dangerous activity, (report it / prevent it) immediately.
5

Complete the outline. Use the words in the box.

Don't use a gas stove for heat.	Don't go outside.
Teach them to dial 911.	In case of a fire:
If you are outside:	~~Turn off electrical equipment.~~

FAMILY EMERGENCY PLAN

I. **In case of a blackout:**
   A. Turn off electrical equipment.
   B. Leave one light on to indicate when power has been turned on.
   C. _____ Its fumes can be poisonous if you breathe them in.
   D. Keep flashlights and batteries in the kitchen.

II. _____
   A. Make sure everyone knows how to use a fire extinguisher.
   B. Make a map of the house showing evacuation routes.
   C. Make sure children know how to call for help:
      1. _____
      2. Teach them at least two phone numbers of family or friends.

III. **In case of an earthquake:**
   A. If you are at home:
      1. _____
      2. Stay away from mirrors and windows.
   B. _____
      1. Stay away from trees.
      2. Stand in a doorway if there's a building nearby.

A Complete the sentences. Use *must* or *must not*.

1. We __must not__ go swimming now.
   They just put chemicals in the pool.

2. We _____ teach the children to
   swim. They'll be safer.

3. The pool deck is wet and slippery.
   You _____ run there.

4. They _____ take glass bottles near
   the pool. That's dangerous.

5. You _____ wear a hat. The sun is really hot.

6. The lifeguard _____ watch the children when they are in the water.

B Write sentences with *has/have to* or *doesn't/don't have to*. Use the words in parentheses.

1. We have a good first-aid kit. (buy another one)

   We don't have to buy another one.

2. You work with dangerous chemicals. (wear gloves)

   _____

3. She's using an iron with a frayed cord. (get a new one)

   _____

4. He has a small cut on his hand. (call 911)

   _____

5. I know exactly how to get out of the city. (use a map)

   _____

6. They heard something about wildfires in the area. (listen for the warnings)

   _____

7. She is driving in the rain. (drive slowly)

   _____

8. He feels an earthquake. (stay inside)

   _____

C Read the list. Write sentences with *had to* (✔) or *didn't have to* (✗).

> 1. buy a new first-aid kit ✔
> 2. get batteries for the radio ✗
> 3. learn about evacuation routes ✗
> 4. bring in all the furniture from the yard ✔
> 5. put their bicycles in the garage ✔

1. They had to buy a new first-aid kit.

2. _____

3. _____

4. _____

5. _____

D Study the Grammar note. Then rewrite the sentences. Use reported speech with *said* or *told*.

> **Grammar note: Reported speech with *must***
>
> Change *must* to *had to* in reported speech in the past.
>
> | **Quoted speech** | **Reported speech** |
> |---|---|
> | "We **must get** a new lamp." | Sven said (that) they **had to get** a new lamp. |
> | "Workers **must wear** hard hats." | He said (that) the workers **had to wear** hard hats. |

1. Karl said, "I must clean up my work area."

   Karl said (that) he had to clean up his work area.

2. The manager told Karl, "You must remove the boxes from the hallway."

   _____

3. Karl said, "I must use a ladder for that job."

   _____

4. The manager told the employees, "You must be careful with flammable liquids."

   _____

A **Complete the conversation. Use the words in the box.**

~~Now we've got a few problems.~~	The streetlight is broken.
The floor is slippery.	We've got to report it so we can cook.
Anyway, I'll take care of it.	There's a problem with the front door lock.

Myra: OK, we're finished moving in.

Now we've got a few problems.
₁

I'm making a list.

Emilio: OK. There is a frayed cord on the stove.

_____
2

Myra: Here's the next item.

_____
3

Emilio: You're right. You know, I tried to fix it myself. I should have called the locksmith.

Myra: I noticed there's a leak in the bathroom.

_____
4

Emilio: Really? I hadn't noticed that.

_____
5

Myra: Do you think we should park the car on the street?

Emilio: No, I guess not. _____
6

We should probably report it.

B **Look at A. Write sentences. Use _should have_ or _shouldn't have_.**

1. Emilio tried to fix the lock himself.

   He shouldn't have tried to fix the lock himself.

2. The repairman didn't fix the stove.

   _____

3. Myra didn't tell Emilio about the leak in the bathroom.

   _____

4. Emilio parked on the street.

   _____

A Read the article. How can we keep small children safe in cars?

○ ○ ○

Making Cars Safer for Children

The most common accident for children is in a car. To prevent serious injury, it is important to make cars safe for them. Before the 1970s, cars were more dangerous for children than they are now. Children rode in the front or the back seat. They did not have to wear seat belts, and few people used child-safety seats. Over the last 50 years, there have been many changes that make cars safer for children.

First, people realized that seat belts did not protect small children. In the 1970s, the government made TV ads announcing that children need child-safety seats. Between 1978 and 1984, all 50 states in the U.S. passed laws that required drivers to use child-safety seats. Since then, safety seats have become better. Seats for children age 0-2 are now designed to face the rear of the car to prevent babies or infants from flying forward after sudden stops.

When air bags[1] became standard in all cars during the 1990s, everyone realized that front-seat air bags were dangerous for small children. Most states have now passed laws that say children under the age of 8 must ride in the back seat of the car. They also recommend that children under the age of 13 ride in the back seat of the car, but they still don't have to in most states. Although some parents still do not obey these laws, they are important. They save the lives of hundreds of children every year.

[1] air bag: a bag in a car that fills with air in an accident to protect the driver and passengers

B Look at A. Mark the sentences *T* (true), *F* (false), or *NI* (no information)

__F__ 1. In 1960, the law said children had to wear seat belts.

_____ 2. The government said that seat belts were better than child-safety seats.

_____ 3. By 1984, children in all 50 states had to use child-safety seats.

_____ 4. In most states, a seven-year-old child has to ride in the back seat.

_____ 5. In the 1990s, people realized air bags were safe for small children.

_____ 6. Before the 1980s, child-safety seats were more expensive.

A Read the handbook. What is its purpose?

Rye County Schools Employee Handbook

CLASSROOM SECURITY

- When leaving the classroom or other work areas between classes or at the end of the day, teachers must turn out the lights and lock all doors. Windows should also be locked at the end of the day.

- Employees must not keep personal items of value in or on their desks. Teachers should tell students not to bring valuable items to school. The district will not be responsible for the loss of, or damage to, personal property due to such causes as fire, theft, accident, or vandalism.

- All teachers have to follow these rules:

  1. They must not make copies of keys.
  2. They must not leave keys on desks or tables, or in mailboxes.
  3. They should not give keys to students except in an emergency.

HEALTH AND SAFETY

- Staff members must report all injuries immediately to the person in charge.

- All materials that might cause someone to slip or fall should be removed from floors or other areas immediately.

- All work areas and hallways have to be free of unnecessary objects.

- Staff members must report hazardous conditions as soon as possible.

B Look at A. Complete these tasks.

1. What are two things that teachers *must not* do with keys?

   make copies _____

   _____

2. Find two sentences with *have to* and circle them.

3. What are two things that staff members must report?

   _____

   _____

4. Read the following sentences. Then write sentences with *should have* or *should not have*.

   a. Mr. Kaufman lent his keys to a student.

   _____

   b. Ms. Franklin didn't lock the window before she left the classroom.

   _____

6 Getting Ahead

LESSON 1 VOCABULARY

A Match the numbers with the parts of the conversation.

Manager: **(1)** I thought we should have this team meeting to think of some suggestions for the problems we've had recently.

Fran: **(2)** Well, I think I should have some training to fix the new photocopier.

Manager: **(3)** Do you mean the color photocopier?

Fran: Yes, that one. The color copier wasn't working yesterday, and Kurt didn't have time to fix it. I was late with an important job.

Kurt: I see your point, Fran, but you know it's difficult to fix these machines. **(4)** You'd need a lot of training.

Fran: Yeah, I guess you're right. **(5)** I wasn't thinking about that.

Manager: OK. Here's what I think we should do. **(6)** I'm going to get another color copier. Then if one copier isn't working, you can use the other one.

____ give feedback   ____ ask for clarification   ____ solve a problem

____ make a suggestion   <u>1</u> work on a team   ____ respond to feedback

B Circle the correct adjective.

1. Kurt works well with many different people. He's very (responsible /(tolerant)).

2. Fran has many different skills. She is (flexible / honest).

3. Fran always tells the manager if she makes a mistake. She's (honest / independent).

4. The photocopier often breaks down. It's not very (reliable / honest).

5. Fran wants to get the work done on time. She's very (responsible / tolerant).

6. Fran works well alone. She is (reliable / independent).

A Read the notes. Complete the memo.

Notes
Progress report: new store procedures
New credit card readers
• need to train part-time cashiers
• have been installed
• finish by: end of the week
• trained all full-time cashiers
System for reordering inventory
• need opinions of the assistant managers
• finish by: the 30th
• made some progress
Suggestion: updating our policies for
employee breaks

Memo

To: Ms. Lee

From: Abdul Reddy

Re: Progress report

I would like to update you on my progress with

the ___new store procedures___ we discussed at our meeting last month.
       1

The new credit card readers have arrived and _____.
                                                              2

I am training all of the cashiers to work with them. All of the

_____ have been trained. I still need to
              3

_____ part-time cashiers from the deli and bakery. I plan
              4

to do that by the _____.
                              5

I have also been working on our _____. I have
                                                    6

_____, but I still need the _____ of
              7   8

the assistant managers. I expect to finish this by _____.
                                                                          9

I would like to work on _____ for employee breaks.
                                          10

I think that we need to make some changes. If you approve, I will take the

initiative on this and give you some recommendations for changes.

I appreciate your feedback. Please let me know if you have any questions.

B Look at A. Circle *a* or *b*.

1. One thing Abdul has already done is _____.

   a. talked to the assistant managers   (b.) installed the new credit card readers

2. One thing Abdul still needs to do is _____.

   a. train the full-time cashiers   b. train the part-time cashiers

3. One thing Abdul suggested is _____.

   a. updating policies on employee breaks   b. getting new credit card readers

4. Abdul plans to finish the new system for reordering inventory by _____.

   a. the end of the week   b. the 30th

A Underline the adjective clause in the sentences. Then complete each clause with *who, which,* or *that.*

1. Ms. Evers is a manager _____who_____ <u>respects her employees and tries to help them.</u>

2. These are a few of the things _____ are important to her in an employee.

3. She likes employees _____ are organized and reliable.

4. She promotes people _____ are responsible and independent.

5. At meetings, Ms. Evers makes comments _____ are helpful and not too long.

6. She knows that everyone prefers team meetings _____ are short!

B Combine the sentences. Use *who, which,* or *that* with adjective clauses.

1. Read this letter from the manager. She can solve the problem.

   _Read this letter from the manager who can solve the problem._____

2. The paychecks were in the envelope. It was in your mailbox.

   _____

3. The employees congratulated their co-worker. He was promoted to manager.

   _____

4. The company offers training courses to employees. They want to learn new skills.

   _____

5. The customer gave the feedback. It was shared with the team.

   _____

6. Marco is the new employee. He sits next to me.

   _____

7. The manager summarized the recommendation. The employees made it.

   _____

C Read the sentences. Underline the adjective clauses. Then write answers to the questions.

1. The photocopier <u>which was installed yesterday</u> is already broken!

   What's broken? _____the photocopier_____

2. The manager who was responsible solved the problem.

   Who solved the problem?_____

3. The human resources assistant who is in charge of payroll noticed the error.

   Who noticed the error? _____

4. The team that had the best interpersonal skills won the award.

   Who won the award? _____

5. At the staff meeting which was held last Tuesday, Fran made a suggestion.

   Where did Fran make a suggestion? _____

6. The employees that use the machine need to be trained.

   Who needs to be trained? _____

7. The job applicant that speaks several languages was hired for the job.

   Who was hired for the job? _____

D Study the Grammar note. Match the parts of the sentences.

> **Grammar note: Adjective clauses in definitions**
>
> Adjective clauses are often used in definitions.
>
> *An **employee** is a person <u>who works for a company or another person</u>.*
> *A **vocational school** is a school <u>that trains students to do specific jobs</u>.*

___b___ 1. An auto mechanic is a person   a. that students can take without a teacher.

_____ 2. A job counselor is a person   b. who fixes cars.

_____ 3. A self-study course is a course   c. that gives a student money for education.

_____ 4. A scholarship is an award   d. who gives advice about work and jobs.

_____ 5. A photocopier is a machine   e. who works from home.

_____ 6. A telecommuter is an employee   f. that makes copies.

DO THE MATH Go to page 89.

A **Complete the conversation. Use the sentences in the box.**

| Sure. Who is Cherise?   Oh, yeah, I know who you mean. Thanks. |
| What should I do?   ~~Who should I see?~~ |

Ramiro: Hi, Gerard. How's your first day going? Do you need something?

Gerard: Uh-huh. I need the keys to the equipment storeroom. <u>Who should I see?</u>

1
Mr. Torval?

Ramiro: No, don't ask Mr. Torval. He's the owner. He doesn't take care of little things like that. Where's Liz, your co-worker? She had the keys this morning.

Gerard: She's on break. _____

2

Ramiro: Go see Cherise. She knows where another set of keys are.

Gerard: _____

3

Ramiro: Cherise is the woman whose desk is near the front. She's Mr. Torval's assistant.

Gerard: _____

4

B **Look at A. Complete the chart.**

Supervisor	New Employee	Owner	Co-worker	Assistant
Ramiro				

C **Combine the sentences. Use *whose*.**

1. Gerard is the new employee. His job is to wash cars.
   <u>Gerard is the new employee whose job is to wash cars.</u>

2. Lydia is the customer. Her car is at the car wash.

   _____

3. Mr. Torval is the owner. His assistant is Cherise.

   _____

4. Ramiro is the supervisor. His team does the most work.

   _____

A Read the article. If you have a conflict at work, who should you talk to first?

Dealing with Conflict at Work

If you are having a conflict with a co-worker, you should try to deal with the problem right away. Don't wait until someone gets angry. It might be helpful to discuss the problem first with someone who is not involved. For example, ask a family member or a friend outside the office for advice. This will give you some ideas about how to talk to your co-worker.

Next, try to discuss the problem with your co-worker. Be friendly, polite, and professional. Explain the problem and make some suggestions for solving it. Then ask for feedback. Listen carefully and try to understand your co-worker's ideas. Remember to be tolerant and flexible. Try to find a solution that both of you are comfortable with.

If you feel you can't talk to your co-worker, or if nothing changes after your meeting, don't give up. Talk to your supervisor. A supervisor can often explain workplace procedures. He or she should also be able to ask for changes in employee behavior without causing problems between employees.

B Look at A. Circle *a* or *b*.

1. When there's a conflict at work, you should _____.

   (a.) solve it quickly   b. get angry

2. When you talk to your co-worker, you should _____.

   a. be tolerant   b. demand immediate changes

3. You should work on a solution _____.

   a. that you like   b. that everyone agrees on

4. If nothing changes after your meeting with your co-worker, you should _____.

   a. give up   b. talk to your supervisor

A Read the story. How was Ernesto's first day on the job?

My First Day on the Job
by Ernesto Guerra

I was very happy Lansley's Department Store had given me my first job. But by the end of the first day, I wished I had paid more attention to the 15-hour training course. First, my manager, Jerry, asked me to work in the kitchen department. That was a problem because I know nothing about pots and pans and all that stuff. My first customer was Mrs. Ramirez. She was very nice, but she had a question. So I went to ask Jerry. When I returned, there were three more customers waiting in line. The second customer, a young man named Mel Reynolds, had a credit card. Then just my luck, the credit-card machine <u>that they had given me</u> wasn't working.

By this time, another customer was getting annoyed and making comments. I started to get very nervous. Finally Sonia, a cashier who was working in the food department, hurried over to help me. She told them it was my first day. Then Jerry gave each customer a 10-percent-off coupon. Suddenly, the customers changed. They told me I shouldn't feel bad at all and I was doing a great job. The customer whose name was Mr. Bernardo said, "You know, they shouldn't have left you alone on such a busy day!"

B Look at A. One adjective clause is underlined. Find two more and underline them.

C Complete the sentences. Use the names and roles in the story.

1. __Mrs. Ramirez__ was the ___customer___ who asked the question.

2. _____ was the _____ who gave the customers coupons.

3. _____ was the young _____ who had a credit card.

4. _____ was the _____ that worked in the food department.

5. _____ was the _____ who said they shouldn't have left Ernesto alone.

A Complete the chart. Use the words and amounts in the box. Use the TOTALS to check your work.

savings – $3,500	~~auto insurance – $900~~	Q-card (credit card) – $2,400
income – $47,000	auto loan – $1,300	health insurance – $2,500
home loan – $105,000	home insurance – $1,400	student loan – $9,500
~~car – $6,000~~	house – $150,000	

Luis and Ximena (Personal finances)					
Assets		**Debts**		**Insurance policies**	
Item	Value	Loan	Amount	Type	Premium (1 year)
car	$6,000			auto insurance	$900
TOTAL	$206,500	**TOTAL**	$118,200	**TOTAL**	$4,800

B Circle the correct words.

Luis and Ximena wanted to buy a new car, so they reviewed their personal finances. Their yearly ((income) / expense) from ₁ their jobs is about $47,000 a year. They also checked their (fixed / variable) expenses, such as their utility bills and ₂ what they spend on food, travel, and entertainment. Their (fixed / variable) expenses include the mortgage payment on their (house / car) and the ₃ ₄ (income / insurance premiums) on their house and car every year. Then Ximena said, "Let's ₅ not forget all the (fixed / miscellaneous) expenses for different little things we buy every ₆ month." So after looking at all the numbers, Ximena and Luis decided they should wait and buy a car next year!

A Read the outline. Then match the sentences with the paragraphs.
Write *P1*, *P2*, or *P3*.

> Neither a borrower, nor a lender be.

Topic: Borrowing and lending
Outline: Paragraph 1: Introduction. Define quotation.
Paragraph 2: Discuss problems with borrowing and lending.
Paragraph 3: Explain why borrowing and lending are sometimes necessary.

Sentences:

_P3_ Some things, like a home or a car, are very expensive.

_P2_ People often borrow too much money, and then they can't pay it back.

____ Most people could not buy these items if they didn't borrow money.

____ Borrowing and lending also creates problems between friends.

____ It means people should never borrow or lend anything.

____ People get angry if a friend doesn't return something they've borrowed.

B Look at A. Complete the essay. Use the sentences in A. Then explain why you agree or disagree with Shakespeare's advice in paragraph 4.

Borrowing and Lending

"Neither a borrower, nor a lender be" is famous advice.

Borrowing and lending can cause problems.

It's true that borrowing and lending can cause problems, but both are sometimes necessary.

I think Shakespeare's advice is ...

A Read the ad. Complete the paragraph. Use the present unreal conditional and the information in the ad.

Buy Your Car from MR. GOODBUY!

New Condo Vista!
Five-passenger family car
$219 per mo./27 mos.
34 mpg*

Taxes not included. $5,000 due at signing.
*mpg = miles per gallon

Pre-owned Sport 6!
Six-passenger van
Excellent condition! Air-conditioned
$159 per mo./36 mos.
22 mpg*

Taxes not included. $3,000 due at signing.

Luis and Ximena have decided they can't buy a car now. If they

_____bought_____ (buy) the Condo Vista, they ___would have___ (have) to pay
  1   2

_____ a month. If they _____ (get) the Sport 6, the monthly
      3   4

payment _____ (be) just _____ a month, but they'd have to pay
              5   6

for _____ months! Also if they _____ (have) the Sport 6, they
        7   8

_____ (spend) more money for gas. They were thinking about the Vista,
      9

but the small print said they had to pay _____ when they signed the
                                                10

contract! Ximena said, "We always read the small print. If we _____ (not
                                                                    11

do) that, we _____ (be) in trouble!"
                  12

B Combine the sentences. Use the present unreal conditional.

1. I don't have enough money. I won't buy that blue car.

   If I had _enough money, I would buy that blue car_____.

2. We don't have car insurance. I can't drive the car.

   If we had _____.

3. We save money every month. We can take a vacation every year.

   But, if we didn't _____.

4. He pays the bills on time. He doesn't have to pay late fees.

   If he didn't _____.

C Complete the questions and answers. Use the present unreal conditional and the verbs in parentheses.

1. **A:** If Gary _____had_____ enough money, would he _____go_____ to college? (have, go)

   B: Yes, he ___would___. He wants to go.

2. **A:** How much _____ it _____ if he _____ to a community college? (cost, go)

   B: It _____ more than $5,000. (cost)

3. **A:** _____ he _____ in school if he _____ a part-time job? (stay, find)

   B: Yes, I think he _____.

4. **A:** If he _____, _____ he _____ better grades? (not work, get)

   B: Probably. He _____ more time to study. (have)

5. **A:** If we _____ him, _____ he _____ hard? (help, work)

   B: Of course, he _____.

D Study the Grammar note. Then complete the conversation with real or unreal conditionals. Use the verbs in parentheses.

> **Grammar note: Real vs. present unreal conditionals**
>
> | **Real conditionals . . .** | **Unreal conditionals . . .** |
> |---|---|
> | • use the present in the *if* clause. | • use the past in the *if* clause. |
> | • use *will* in the main clause. | • use *would* in the main clause. |
> | *If I go on the trip, I'll enjoy it.* | *If I went on the trip, I'd enjoy it.* |

Terry: If I decide to buy a house, I_____'ll try_____ to get a bank loan. (try)
                                                                    1

Pat: If you apply for a loan, you _____ a few weeks. (have to wait)
                                              2

Terry: I'll be lucky if I _____ a house in a good neighborhood. (find)
                                    3

Pat: Hmm. If you bought an old house and fixed it up, it _____ cheaper. (be)
                                                                          4

Terry: Yes, it would be cheaper if I _____ the work myself. (do)
                                                5

Pat: If you had to pay people to do the work, it _____ too expensive. (be)
                                                              6

Terry: If I were a millionaire, I _____ so much! (not have to worry)
                                              7

A **Complete the conversation. Use the sentences in the box.**

> How about if we go on Monday afternoon? Business Mart is 30 miles away.
>
> Well, what if we shop there once a month? When do you want to go?
>
> ~~You know, we shouldn't buy so much there.~~

Jon: We need a few things for the coffee shop. I think I'll go to that store on the corner.

Yen: <u>You know, we shouldn't buy so much there.</u> It's expensive.
                                   1

Jon: If I went to Business Mart, we'd save money.

Yen: _____ You don't have time to drive that far
                                   2

every week.

Jon: _____ We could buy most of our supplies there.
                                   3

Yen: That's a good idea. _____
                                             4

Jon: _____
                                   5

Yen: OK. The shop isn't very busy on Mondays.

B **Look at A. Combine the sentences. Use the unreal conditional with _be_. Use the negative in one of the clauses.**

1. The prices are too high. Jon and Yen won't shop at the local store.

   <u>If the prices weren't too high, Jon and Yen would shop at the local store.</u>

2. Business Mart is so far away. They won't drive there every week.

   _____

3. The prices at Business Mart aren't high. They will shop there.

   _____

4. Jon and Yen are busy. They won't go to Business Mart more often.

   _____

5. The coffee shop isn't busy on Mondays. They will have time to go shopping.

   _____

DO THE MATH Go to page 90.

A Read the article. Who do you think this advice is good for?

○ ● ○

Money Manners

Different cultures often have different ideas about what is polite when talking about money. In the U.S., for example, people often consider income and financial topics to be private. It is not considered good manners to ask a direct question about someone's salary.

Wow! This is nice stuff. How much did it cost?

Even good friends often do not share this information with each other. In the workplace, you should only discuss your salary with your supervisor. Many companies protect employee salary information.

Also, it is best not to ask what things cost. For example, when visiting someone's home, it is fine to say that you like their furniture or something they are wearing. However, it is not a good idea to ask how much these things cost. This is especially true of expensive items, such as a car or a house.

If someone asks you about your income, you don't have to answer the question. For example, you could say with a smile something like, "If I told you, you'd be surprised" or "I'd really rather not say." If you really needed to know how much someone paid for a small item, you could say, "Excuse me, but would you mind telling me how much that cost? I'll understand if you don't want to tell me."

B Look at A. Mark the statements and questions as *A* (appropriate) or *NA* (not appropriate) in a social conversation.

_NA_ 1. Hi, Joe. Tell me, how much is the company paying you these days?

_____ 2. Wow! I like this TV. The picture's really clear.

_____ 3. Great house, Mary! How much did you pay for it?

_____ 4. I'd really rather not talk about my salary right now.

_____ 5. This is a nice tablet. Would you mind if I asked how much it cost?

Complete the sentences. Use the present unreal conditional and your own ideas.

If I . . .

If I had more time on the weekend, I would go for a walk on the beach.

1. If I had more time on the weekend,

   I _____.

2. If I were in the supermarket and saw someone stealing food,

   I _____.

3. If I could be anything I wanted to,

   I _____.

4. If I found $100 on a bus,

   I _____.

5. If I had time to take another class,

   I _____.

6. If I ever had the courage,

   I _____.

7. If I had the chance to visit any country in the world,

   I _____.

8. If I designed my own house,

   it _____.

9. If I were able to _____,

   I _____.

10. If I had a chance to meet someone famous,

    I _____.

11. If I lived near _____,

    I _____.

12. If I had the chance to change one thing in my life,

    I _____.

A Circle the correct words.

Rosa: What is all this, Viki? Are you having a (yard sale / thrift store) today?
₁

Viki: Uh-huh. Remember this old chair? We bought it at the Saturday
(thrift store / flea market) downtown.
₂

Rosa: Yeah, we had a good time that day. Why are you selling this beautiful table?
Oh, I see. It's scratched.

Viki: It was always scratched. I bought it (as is / online) from that discount furniture
₃
store for $25.

Rosa: Do you want to go to the sale at Markham's Jewelry store tomorrow? Everything is
(as is / on clearance).
₄

Viki: No, thanks. I don't like crowds. It's easier to use my computer to shop the
(online stores / yard sales).
₅

B Write the correct words under the pictures. Use the words in the box.

| stained | dented | torn | ~~scratched~~ | faded | defective |

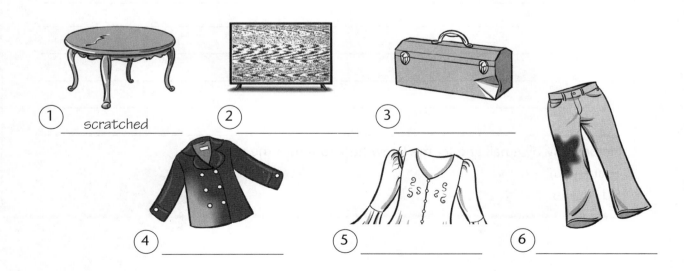

1 _____scratched_____

2 _____

3 _____

4 _____

5 _____

6 _____

A Read the outline. Then match the sentences with the paragraphs.
Write *P1, P2,* or *P3.*

Topic: Order problem with Harry's Discount Electronics

Outline: Paragraph 1: Say where and when the camera was bought.
Say there's a problem.

Paragraph 2: Explain the problem.

Paragraph 3: Say what you want the company to do.

Sentences:

_P2_ First, the camera is defective. It doesn't zoom.

_P1_ I ordered a Sanvey 200 SLR camera from your online store on March 2.

_____ If you cannot fix the camera, please send me a new one.

_____ I received the camera on March 6, but there are some problems with
the order.

_____ Second, the price of the camera was $299.00, but on the bill, I was charged
$350.00.

_____ Finally, I would like a new bill for the correct amount.

B Complete the email to Harry's Discount Electronics. Use the sentences in A.

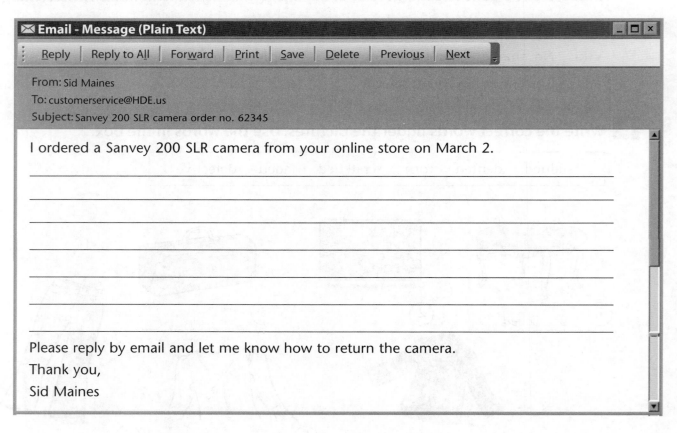

✉ **Email - Message (Plain Text)**   _ □ ×

Reply | Reply to All | Forward | Print | Save | Delete | Previous | Next

From: Sid Maines
To: customerservice@HDE.us
Subject: Sanvey 200 SLR camera order no. 62345

I ordered a Sanvey 200 SLR camera from your online store on March 2.

_____

_____

_____

_____

_____

_____

Please reply by email and let me know how to return the camera.

Thank you,

Sid Maines

A **Complete the sentences. Use the *-ing* or the *-ed* form of the adjectives in parentheses.**

1. We were _____surprised_____ when our cousin invited us to go shopping in the city. (surprise)

2. When we arrived, she was _____ to see us. (excite)

3. Everyone was _____ about where to go, but we finally found some good stores. (confuse)

4. We had an _____ time shopping at a flea market. (interest)

5. On the last day, the weather was _____. It started raining. (disappoint)

6. I had a great time. It's never _____ downtown in the big city! (bore)

B **Complete sentences with the *-ed* or *-ing* form of the underlined verb.**

1. The first view of the island <u>excited</u> everyone.

   a. The first view of the island was _____exciting_____.

   b. Everyone was _____excited_____.

2. But the shopping trip <u>disappointed</u> the tourists.

   a. The shopping trip was _____.

   b. The tourists were _____.

3. The prices <u>surprised</u> them.

   a. They were _____.

   b. The prices were _____.

4. The stores didn't <u>interest</u> us.

   a. The shops weren't _____.

   b. We weren't _____.

5. The directions <u>confused</u> him.

   a. He was _____.

   b. The directions were _____.

C Circle the correct adjectives.

Eric was (boring / (bored)) with his usual everyday schedule. He wanted to have
an (excited / exciting) weekend. He wasn't (interested / interesting) in the
usual TV shows. He thought the traffic and the people at the shopping mall
were (annoyed / annoying). He decided to go on a long, (relaxing / relaxed)
weekend in the mountains. Out in the country, Eric was (surprised / surprising)
by the beautiful scenery. He was (comforted / comforting) by the clean, fresh
air. He had a great time and took lots of (interested / interesting) pictures.

D Circle the correct adverbs.

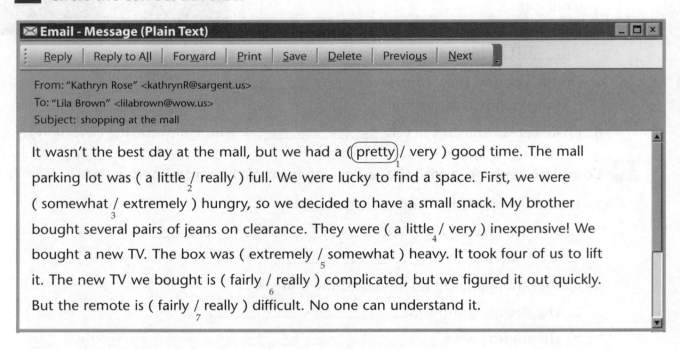

Email - Message (Plain Text)

Reply | Reply to All | Forward | Print | Save | Delete | Previous | Next

From: "Kathryn Rose" <kathrynR@sargent.us>
To: "Lila Brown" <lilabrown@wow.us>
Subject: shopping at the mall

It wasn't the best day at the mall, but we had a ((pretty) / very) good time. The mall
parking lot was (a little / really) full. We were lucky to find a space. First, we were
(somewhat / extremely) hungry, so we decided to have a small snack. My brother
bought several pairs of jeans on clearance. They were (a little / very) inexpensive! We
bought a new TV. The box was (extremely / somewhat) heavy. It took four of us to lift
it. The new TV we bought is (fairly / really) complicated, but we figured it out quickly.
But the remote is (fairly / really) difficult. No one can understand it.

E Complete the sentences. Use your own ideas.

I've always been very interested in computers.

1. I've always been very interested in _____.

2. _____ is the most exciting movie I've ever seen.

3. The students were excited when _____.

4. I think that _____ is very boring.

5. English can be very confusing when _____.

DO THE MATH Go to page 90.

A **Complete the conversation. Use the words and phrases in the box.**

confirmation number	disappointing	free breakfast
How may I help you?	I'm afraid not	Unfortunately

A: Seaside Inn. Kelly speaking. _____?
1

B: Hello. I made a reservation and asked for a room with a view, but the email confirmation says I have no view.

A: OK, let's see if I can help you. What's the _____?
2

B: Let's see. It's 429901.

A: Ms. Gonzalez?

B: Yes, that's me.

A: Okay, I see your reservation.

_____, there are no
3
rooms with a view left on the 19th.

B: But I made my reservation weeks ago. You can't change my room?

A: No, _____. Those rooms are very popular. They are usually
4
reserved months in advance.

B: Well, that's _____.
5

A: Yes, I understand. I will send you a coupon for a _____ for two
6
at our Seaside Restaurant as a way to say sorry.

B: That would be great. Thank you.

B **Look at A. Write answers to the questions. Use complete sentences.**

1. What kind of room does the caller want?

_____

2. What does the hotel clerk offer to give the caller?

_____

3. Does the caller keep her reservation at the hotel?

_____

C **Complete the sentences. Use _so, such,_ or _such a_.**

1. The Seaside Restaurant was _____so_____ crowded that we couldn't get a table.

2. We went to that Chinese restaurant that had _____ good review in the paper.

3. They had _____ good fish that everyone ordered it.

4. It was _____ late by the time we got back that I couldn't call you.

A Read the article. What's the largest online auction site?

Online Auctions: A Global Marketplace

Online auctions make it possible for ordinary people to buy and sell things on the Internet. Here's how an auction works. Imagine that you want to sell a chair. You write a description of the chair and take a picture of it. Then you put the picture "up" on an auction website. You also decide on an opening price for the chair—let's say $5.00. Now people can go online and see your chair and all of this information.

Person A sees your chair and likes it, so he or she makes a bid—an offer to buy the chair at a certain price—for example, $10.00. Then Person B sees the chair and also wants to make a bid. This person has to bid more than $10.00, so he or she might bid $15.00. It goes on like this until the time for the auction is over. Each person who makes a bid has to bid more than the previous bidder. You then sell the chair to the highest bidder. If you're lucky, you'll get a good price for your chair.

The largest online auction site, eBay, started in 1995. It now has a membership of more than 150 million people. It is extremely popular all over the world. There are local websites in various countries in Europe, Asia, Australia, and South America. People buy and sell all kinds of things online, from books to cars to houses and many unusual items as well. One woman even wanted to "sell" her husband on eBay! But eBay said, "No! You can't do that."

B Look at A. Mark the sentences *T* (true), *F* (false), or *NI* (no information).

__T__ 1. You don't have to be an official business person to sell things online.

_____ 2. A *bid* is an offer to sell something at a certain price.

_____ 3. In an auction, there is a limited number of bidders.

_____ 4. Millions of people are now buying and selling things on eBay.

_____ 5. You can buy a husband or wife on eBay.

A Read the catalog. What would be a good name for this store?

Heavy-duty, waterproof flashlight
<u>Long-lasting</u> batteries (150 hours)

Woman's business suit with fitted jacket
Matching blouse also available

Convenient, folding baby stroller
Beautifully (decorated) with your child's
favorite characters

Delicious, naturally flavored fruit bars!
Each box contains 8 individually
packaged bars

Blue jeans, just the right faded look!
Relaxed fit, great-looking

Men's shoes
Designed for comfort

B Look at A. Complete the tasks.

1. One adjective ending in *-ing* is underlined. Find three more and underline them.

2. One adjective ending in *-ed* is circled. Find six more and circle them.

A Look at the flyer. Write the correct words under each picture. Then complete the paragraph. Use the words in the box.

active lifestyle	good nutrition	heredity
~~yearly physicals~~	prenatal care	dental checkups

Five Keys to Good Health

yearly physicals				
1	2	3	4	5

Your _____, or family history, is also an important
                                                    6
part of your health history. It's important to have regular medical screenings
for conditions that are common in your family.
Early detection can save your life!

B Circle the correct words.

1. She has mild but (severe /(chronic)) headaches, two or three every month.

2. The doctor asked if you are (allergic / chronic) to any foods.

3. From your (symptoms / allergies), I would say you probably have a cold.

4. Diabetes is becoming a common childhood (disease / weakness).

5. He's had some (disease / weakness) in that arm since he broke it last year.

LESSON 2 WRITING

A Read the email. Complete the paragraphs with the phrases in the box.

> My advice to you is to start a low-salt diet.
> She said I should exercise at least three times a week.
> ~~I went to the doctor last week for a checkup.~~
> mine is a little high, too.
> and I have more energy

To: Gloria Tomas <gtomas 123@umail.com>
From: Teresa Tomas <teresatomas@umail.com>
Subject: RE: checking in

Dear Gloria,

Thanks for your email. I'm glad to hear that you had such a good time on your vacation.

Everything's OK here. <u>I went to the doctor last week for a checkup.</u> She said I'm
                                                    1

in good health, but I have to lose a little weight. _____
                                                                        2

Well, I now walk every morning for 30 minutes, and so far, I've lost two pounds

_____!
            3

You said that your blood pressure is high. _____ I am
                                                            4

doing the same because _____ No more salty potato chips
                                    5

for me!

We're all looking forward to seeing you when you come next month.

Love from your sister,

Teresa

B Look at A. Write answers to the questions. Use complete sentences.

1. What did the doctor say about Teresa's weight? <u>She has to lose a little weight.</u>

2. How does Teresa exercise? _____

3. What's the problem with Gloria's blood pressure? _____

4. What is Teresa's advice to Gloria? _____

A Complete the sentences. Use the affirmative or negative forms of the words in parentheses.

1. Debra _____shouldn't cancel_____ her doctor's appointment. (should, cancel)

2. Debra and Jon _____ every day. (ought to, exercise)

3. Jon has high blood pressure. He _____ a lot of salty food. (had better, eat)

4. Debra _____ any weight at this time. (should, lose)

5. Debra _____ a lot of rest. (should, get)

6. Jon _____ sugar. (ought to, cut out)

B Unscramble the sentences.

1. blood test / Debra / tomorrow / has a

   _Debra has a blood test tomorrow._____

2. nervous / She / shouldn't / the test / feel / about

   _____

3. said that / anything after / she had / not / midnight / better / eat / The doctor

   _____

4. ought to / water before / the test / drink some / She

   _____

5. follow all / She had / instructions carefully / doctor's / of the / better

   _____

6. ought / review / Her doctor / to / the test results / her / with

   _____

C Match the sentences with the advice.

__c__ 1. Sergio works too hard.

_____ 2. One day he got sick at work.

_____ 3. Dr. Ana Garcia examined him.

_____ 4. The doctor gave Sergio some advice.

_____ 5. Sergio's boss, Mr. Ward, also gave him some advice.

a. His co-workers said, "You must go to the hospital."

b. She said, "Sergio, you really ought to take a vacation."

c. His children say, "Dad, you should work fewer hours."

d. He said, "Sergio, you've got to stop working so much overtime!"

e. She said, "I'd better do some tests to see what the problem is."

D Mark the sentences *M* (mild), *S* (strong), or *SR* (stronger).

__SR__ 1. You must go to the hospital.

_____ 2. Sergio, you really ought to take a vacation.

_____ 3. Dad, you should work fewer hours.

_____ 4. Sergio, you've got to stop working so much overtime!

_____ 5. You'd better stay in the hospital for a couple of days.

E Find the error in the underlined part of each sentence. Then rewrite the sentence correctly.

1. <u>I've got wait</u> a long time to see the doctor.

   I've got to wait a long time to see the doctor.

2. You <u>must to take</u> some time off.

   _____

3. You <u>ought go</u> to the pharmacy right away.

   _____

4. You <u>had not better take</u> that medication without a prescription.

   _____

5. He <u>shouldn't to leave</u> the hospital.

   _____

A Complete Teresa's part of the conversation. Use the phrases in the box.

> What else do you recommend?
>
> What can I do to lower my blood pressure?
>
> So I understand that I should eat a lot of fruits and
>   vegetables and cut back on tea and coffee
>
> ~~How's my blood pressure?~~

Doctor: Hi, Teresa. How have you been since your last checkup?

Teresa: I'm a little tired, but I'm OK. _____How's my blood pressure?_____
$\quad$ 1

Doctor: Your blood pressure is still a little high, but it's not too bad.

Teresa: Oh, dear. _____
$\quad$ 2

Doctor: Well, you can eat a lot of fruits and vegetables and cut back on tea and coffee.

Teresa: I see. _____
$\quad$ 3

Doctor: You should try not to worry.

Teresa: _____,
$\quad$ 4
but how am I supposed to stop worrying?

B Complete the sentences. Use the infinitive or gerund form of the verb in parentheses. Check (✓) the sentences that have two possible answers.

_____ 1. When did you decide _____to see_____ the doctor? (see)

_____ 2. How do I know when I need _____ my blood pressure? (check)

_____ 3. The problem is she likes _____ salty foods. (eat)

_____ 4. I'll quit _____ overtime. (work)

_____ 5. You have got to avoid _____ coffee or soda. (drink)

_____ 6. They are planning _____ every day. (exercise)

_____ 7. We prefer _____ outside. (walk)

_____ 8. He'd consider _____ sugar from his diet. (cut)

DO THE MATH Go to page 91.

A Read the article. Why is chocolate good for your health?

Chocolate for Your Health

A box of chocolate is always a good present on Valentine's Day, but did you know that chocolate might be good for you? Doctors have studied members of the Kuna tribe to learn how healthy chocolate is. The Kuna mainly live on islands in the Caribbean Sea. They are very healthy. The Kuna almost never have high blood pressure or heart disease, although they eat a lot of salty food. Interestingly, the Kuna diet includes four or five cups a day of a drink made from raw cocoa. (Chocolate is made from the beans of the cocoa plant.) Doctors think this might be the reason for the Kunas' good health.

The healthy ingredients in cocoa are called flavanols. Flavanols help prevent heart disease. Because flavanols have a bitter[1] taste, most chocolate makers remove them. Milk chocolate and white chocolate, for example, have no flavanols. However, high-quality dark chocolate may have enough flavanols to be good for the heart. Of course, if you don't like dark chocolate, you can always reduce stress and get healthier by living on a beautiful Caribbean island!

[1] bitter: with a bad taste, not sweet

B Look at A. Circle *a* or *b*.

1. The Kuna people mainly live _____.

   a. in a big city   (b.) on islands

2. Doctors believe that the Kunas' good health might be because of _____.

   a. the salty food they eat   b. the cocoa they drink

3. Flavanols have a _____ taste.

   a. bitter   b. sweet

4. _____ chocolate is healthier for you than white chocolate.

   a. Milk   b. Dark

A Read the form.

HEALTH HISTORY

PLEASE PRINT

Name: Yoon   Ben   Alan
          Last name   First name   Middle name

Address: 295 Elm Street   Alto Crest   NM 88345   (505) 555-4362
          Street address   City   State/Zip   Phone

Date of birth: 8/26/1972   Place of birth: Utica, New York   Sex: Ⓜ/ F
          Month/day/year

Person to notify in an emergency:
Name / relationship: Emma Thomas/sister   Home phone: (505) 555-5430

Personal Physician: Dr. Mark Perez   22 Main St. Suite 203   (505) 555-6897
          Name   Address   Phone

Allergies: pet hair, chocolate, aspirin

Have you ever had or do you now have any of the following?

	Yes	No		Yes	No		Yes	No
Bone disease		✗	Headaches	✗		Overweight (Obesity)	✗	
Chickenpox	✗		Heart problems		✗	Stomach trouble		✗
Ear disease		✗	High blood pressure	✗		Trouble sleeping	✗	
Eating problem		✗	Lung disease		✗	Hospitalization	✗	
Eye disease		✗	Major injury	✗		Other serious illness		✗

Please explain all YES answers: I had chickenpox when I was 10. I suffer from chronic
headaches (2–3 a month). I take medication for high blood pressure. In 1995, I was in
a car accident, and I broke my left arm and leg. I was in the hospital for 2 weeks.

B Look at A. Write short answers to the questions.

1. What is Mr. Yoon's middle name? __Alan_____

2. Where was he born? _____

3. When was he born? _____

4. Who should they call if there's an emergency? _____

5. What disease did Mr. Yoon have as a child? _____

6. What is Mr. Yoon allergic to? _____

7. What does Mr. Yoon take medication for? _____

8. How did Mr. Yoon break his arm and leg? _____

9. Mr. Yoon didn't explain two of his problems in the notes. Which are they?

    _____

    _____

A Write the correct words under each picture.

> discussed alternatives   developed a plan   implemented the plan
>
> ~~identified a problem~~   proposed a solution

identified a problem

B Match the problems with the departments.

<u> d </u> 1. "There have been a lot of robberies around here." a. Public Works

_____ 2. "I need to work, but I have a two-year-old boy." b. Senior Services

_____ 3. "The streetlight on our corner is broken." c. Parks & Recreation

_____ 4. "We need a lawyer for a problem in our building." d. Public Safety

_____ 5. "I need a nurse to care for my mother." e. Legal Services

_____ 6. "Are there any good summer programs for teens?" f. Childcare Services

A Complete the email. Use the sentences in the box.

> There are also many teenagers and older people here who need transportation.
>
> We would like the city to bring a bus line to our area.
>
> Our community is near the intersection of Field and Mason Streets.

○ ○ ○

To: jkowalski@daviscouncil.mail
From: trwalters@online.met
Subject: Bus Service Needed

Dear Council Member Kowalski:

P1 I am writing to ask for help with a problem in our community.
_____

There is no bus service in this area.

P2 It is a growing area. Many people need a bus service to get to work. _____
_____

P3 _____

You can contact me at 912-555-3490 or at trwalters@online.met.

Sincerely,
Tulia Walters

B Look at A. Answer the questions. Write *P1*, *P2*, or *P3*.

1. Which paragraph says what the writer wants the city to do? _____

2. Which paragraph introduces the problem? _____

3. Which paragraph explains the problem and gives examples? _____

A Mark the questions *D* (direct) or *I* (indirect).

__D__ 1. What's the telephone number of the police station?

_____ 2. How often do they have loud parties like this?

_____ 3. Do you know which apartment the noise is coming from?

_____ 4. Why didn't they invite us?

_____ 5. Can you tell me when the party started?

B Rewrite the questions. Change them from direct to indirect questions. Use the words in parentheses.

1. How many people were there at the party? (Do you know)

    Do you know how many people there were at the party?

2. What are they going to do with all that trash in the parking lot? (Can you tell me)

    _____

3. What time did they leave? (Do you have any idea)

    _____

4. What did the landlord say about the party last night? (Do you know)

    _____

5. When are we having a meeting about the problem? (Could you please tell me)

    _____

C Read the flyer. Then read the direct questions. Complete the indirect questions with *if* or *whether*.

What to Do about Barking Dogs

It is illegal for pet owners to allow dogs to bark in the city of Oceanview.

The city charges fines up to $500.00 for barking dogs.

To report a barking dog problem, call the hotline at (915) 555-2500.

1. Does our building have any rules about pets?

   Do you know _if (whether) our building has any rules about pets_ ?

2. Is it illegal to keep a barking dog?

   Do you know _____?

3. Are there many barking dogs in this neighborhood?

   Do you have any idea _____?

4. Does the city take the dogs away from the owners?

   Can you tell me _____?

5. Is this the right number to call to report the neighbor's barking dog?

   Do you know _____?

D Study the Grammar note. Then read the direct questions. Complete the indirect information and *yes/no* questions.

Grammar note: Indirect questions with *will*	
Direct questions	**Indirect questions**
Will he do **it**?	Can you tell me **if** he **will do** it?
Will Amy **be** there?	Do you know **whether** Amy **will be** there?
When **will** they **come**?	Do you have any idea **when** they**'ll come**?

1. Will the new recreation center have a pool?

   Do you know _whether (if) the new recreation center will have a pool_ ?

2. Will a police officer attend the meeting?

   Can you tell me _____?

3. When will they repair the street near our house?

   Do you know _____?

4. Where will the city put the new traffic light?

   Could you tell me _____?

A **Complete the conversation. Use the sentences in the box.**

> Do you know if people can speak at the meeting?
>
> I'll be there.
>
> ~~I'm calling because I heard the town is making changes to South Street Park.~~
>
> I'm not sure that a recycling center there is a good idea.
>
> I hear what you're saying.

Sunita: City of Alto Plano. Sunita speaking. May I help you?

Tai: My name is Tai Le. <u>I am calling because I heard the town is making changes</u>
<u>to South Street Park.</u> Is this true?
                    1

Sunita: Yes, it is. They're planning to add more parking and a recycling center.

Tai: Hmm... _____
                                    2

Sunita: _____
                         3
We've gotten a lot of calls about this. Listen, there's a public hearing on March 7th.

Tai: Great! _____
                                4

Sunita: Yes, they can. The hearing is from six to nine o'clock in City Hall.

Tai: Thanks. _____
                                5
I have a lot of questions.

B **Circle the correct words.**

1. Tai doesn't know if (are they /(they are)) building a recycling center.

2. She has no idea where (is the meeting / the meeting is).

3. She's not sure when (it starts / does it start).

4. Sally and Juan don't know whether (it is / is it) open to the public.

5. She can't remember if (do they have / they have) plans that night.

6. He forgot where (they plan / do they plan) to build it.

A Read the article. Who do food banks help?

What Is a Food Bank?

A food bank is a community organization that collects free food from farmers, restaurants, and grocery stores before it is thrown out. The food bank then delivers the food at low or no cost to people in need.

Food banks give food to childcare centers, senior centers, and homeless shelters. They bring bags of groceries to older people who cannot leave their homes. Food banks also provide emergency food for low-income people. Families with health or employment problems can receive a week's supply of food within hours of filling out a form asking for food help.

Every year, the food bank, Feeding America, distributes about four billion meals to people in need. It also provides supplies to emergency centers during disasters like earthquakes and hurricanes.

In 2016, they sent more than three million pounds of food, water, and cleaning supplies to the victims of Hurricane Matthew in the U.S.

Food banks are important. They provide a valuable service to the community and prevent the waste of good food that might otherwise be thrown away.

B Look at A. Mark the sentences *T* (true), *F* (false), or *NI* (no information).

_F_ 1. Food banks buy food from restaurants and grocery stores.

____ 2. Childcare centers sometimes receive food from food banks.

____ 3. To get food from a food bank, people have to go to the bank and pick it up.

____ 4. Feeding America gave more than three million meals to the victims of Hurricane Matthew.

____ 5. With food banks, less food is wasted in the U.S.

____ 6. Feeding America also sends a lot of food to other countries.

A Read the report of the public hearing. What was the purpose of the meeting?

Minutes[1] for Public Hearing

Alto Plano City Hall

June 7, 6–9 p.m.

Item 1—Public Hearing: Uses of South Street Park

Senior Development Coordinator J. B. Alvarez explained that the Town of Alto Plano proposed new playing fields, parking areas (called "Parking Gardens"), a dog park, and a recycling center for South Street Park. Mr. Ben Yoon described the site design.

<u>Council Member Vance asked why more parking areas were needed.</u>

Mayor Charles asked what the term "Parking Garden" meant. Mr. Seong responded with a description of the design of car-parking areas.

At this point, the meeting was opened to questions from members of the community.

Ms. Tai Le asked why they were planning a recycling center in this location. Mr. Yoon said the community needed a recycling center and that the park offered the necessary space.

Mr. Robert Greene wasn't sure if the new playing fields were a good idea. He expressed concern about increased noise and activity in the park. He also asked if it was possible to use the playing fields for concerts or other performances. The council agreed to explore the idea of using the playing fields for concerts.

The council then agreed to continue the hearing on August 25.

[1]minutes: an official written report of a meeting

B Look at A. Complete the tasks.

1. Write four things the town is planning to add to South Street Park.

   <u>new playing fields</u> _____

   _____ _____

2. One question reported with the word *asked* is underlined in the minutes. Find three more and underline them.

3. Find a sentence that uses the expression *wasn't sure if* and circle it.

4. Write two things the council agreed to do.

   _____ _____

A Write the parts of the webpage below. Use the words in the box.

| cursor | pointer | pull-down menu | search box | scroll bar | ~~URL box~~ |

1. URL box
2. _____
3. _____
4. _____
5. _____
6. _____

B Look at A. Read the *Links* column. Write the link each person should click on.

1. "I want to find the Frequently Asked Questions." — FAQ
2. "What's the first page of this website?" — _____
3. "I'd like some information about this company." — _____
4. "What's the company's email address or phone number?" — _____
5. "Is there anything new I should look at?" — _____

A **Complete the paragraphs. Use the sentences in the box.**

> However, these days, handwritten messages are still important for some things.
>
> Thirty years ago, most personal letters were written by hand.
>
> Now with so many different electronic devices, it's easy to send an email or instant message.

Writing Letters—Then and Now

_____

It took weeks to write and get a reply. Many people didn't like to write letters. Stamps were expensive, especially for overseas mail.

_____

Emailing individual messages doesn't cost anything. Many people write to each other more frequently since it's more convenient and the messages arrive quickly.

_____

Getting "real" mail is a special treat, so many people prefer sending "real" paper birthday cards by regular mail. They also use regular mail to send custom cards for other occasions, like birth announcements, wedding invitations, and holiday greetings.

B **Complete the essay below. Use the notes on the card.**

Essay Notes
1) listen to radio, go to live concerts
2) can download or stream music from Internet, don't need to go to a store
3) live music more exciting, see artists in "real" life, sound better than recorded

Listening to Music— Then and Now

One hundred years ago, people didn't have many different ways to listen to music. _____

_____

Now people can get music from many different sources. _____

_____

_____

However, many people still like their music "live." _____

_____

_____

A Match the first part of each question with the correct tag.

<u>c</u> 1. The URL for Skyway was www.skyway.us,   a. are you?

____ 2. Your password isn't "pizza,"   b. was it?

____ 3. You're looking at the home page,   c. wasn't it?

____ 4. We aren't traveling on Friday the 13th,   d. weren't you?

____ 5. You were able to make a reservation,   e. is it?

____ 6. You aren't a landlord,   f. aren't you?

____ 7. That Internet connection wasn't fast,   g. are we?

B Complete the conversation. Use tag questions with *be*.

Customer: You're a salesperson, _____<u>aren't you</u>_____?
                                                                     1

Salesman: Yes, I am. How can I help you?

Customer: What's the price of this Bell 560 computer? They're on sale,

_____?
                   2

Salesman: Yes, they are. They're 20 percent off. You weren't interested

in the 750 model, _____?
                                     3

Customer: No, I wasn't, but it *is* nice. They're both equipped with

Internet Star, _____?
                                4

Salesman: Yes, they are. Point the cursor at the red star and click.

That was fast, _____?
                               5

Customer: Yes, it certainly was.

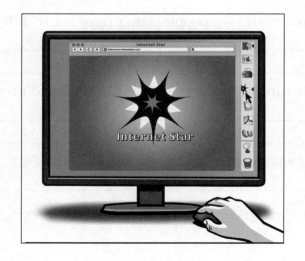

C Complete the questions. Use tag questions with *do, does,* or *did*.

1. We don't have to go to the library today, _____*do we*_____?

2. You didn't save the assignment on your computer, _____?

3. I sent you Julio's email message, _____?

4. She doesn't know how to take photos with her phone, _____?

5. He didn't take the online English class, _____?

D Write short answers to the questions. Agree or disagree.
Follow the words in parentheses.

1. **A:** There isn't any more space in our Internet class, is there? (disagree)

   B: _____*Yes, there is*_____. There's room for one more person.

2. **A:** The teacher shows you how to design webpages, doesn't she? (agree)

   B: _____. That's why I'm taking the class.

3. **A:** We didn't have to sign up for the computer lab, did we? (disagree)

   B: _____. You'd better sign up now before it's too late.

4. **A:** The assignments are on the website, aren't they? (agree)

   B: _____. Go to the website and click on *homework*.

E Study the Grammar note. Then complete the conversation. Use tag
questions with *can* or *will*.

> Grammar note: Tag questions with ***can*** and ***will***
>
> *You'll come,* ***won't you****?*   *He can do it,* ***can't he****?*
> *They won't come,* ***will they****?*   *We can't do it,* ***can we****?*

Arturo: You'll come with us on our trip this weekend, _____*won't you*_____?
                                                                              1

Miguel: What about my research paper? I won't finish it if I go with you,

   _____?
          2

Arturo: You can use my computer to finish the paper tonight,

   _____?
          3

Miguel: Yes, but I'll be trying to write. You'll be having fun,

   _____?
          4

Arturo: No, I have homework, too. We can do it together, _____?
                                                                                    5

A **Complete the conversation. Use the sentences in the box.**

> Uh . . . type what?
>
> Can I suggest something?
>
> Type *open a childcare center*.
>
> ~~Have you found out how to set up a childcare center yet~~?
>
> Here's a whole list of sites.
>
> First, turn on the computer and click on the Internet icon.

Angie: Have you found out how to set up a childcare center yet?
  1

Rosa: No, not yet. I need some help.

Angie: _____
  2

Why don't you look on the Internet?

Rosa: That would be great, but I've never done

it before.

Angie: Let's try it together.

_____
  3

Rosa: What should I type in the search box?

Angie: _____ Then click *Go*.
  4

Rosa: _____
  5

Angie: *Open a childcare center.*

Rosa: Oh, look. _____ This is great. Thanks!
  6

Angie: You're welcome.

B **Match the sentences with the questions.**

_c_ 1. Type *open a childcare center*.   a. Where?

____ 2. Ask Mr. Papadakos to help you.   b. The what?

____ 3. You'd better read the contract carefully.   c. Type what?

____ 4. There are about 50 sites with information.   d. Ask who?

____ 5. I found the information on the Internet.   e. About how many?

DO THE MATH Go to page 92.

A Read the article. What does a search engine do to help you find information on the Internet?

How to Find Useful Websites

What's a search engine?

A search engine is a computer program that searches the Internet for information on certain topics. Each search engine provides a search box for the user to enter keywords, for example, *job search*. The user clicks on the search button, and the search engine looks for pages that contain these words.

How many websites are listed?

There can be thousands, even millions of websites for one topic. One search engine generated more than 1,600,000 hits for the phrase *job search*! (In computer language, people refer to each result of a web search as a *hit*.) However, the most popular sites are usually listed on the first few pages.

How do I find the best website for my topic?

You need to be specific about what you want to find. To look for the words *job search* as a phrase, not as the words *job* and *search* separately, put the phrase in quotation marks, "job search." Then add the type of job you are looking for, for example, *chef*. On the search engine mentioned above, adding the word *chef* reduced the number of hits to a few more than 200,000. To get even fewer, you might add the name of the city where you want work.

B Look at A. Circle *a* or *b*.

1. The words you put in the search box are called _____.

   (a.) keywords   b. a search engine

2. The search for a phrase like *job search* will probably find _____ of websites.

   a. hundreds or thousands   b. thousands or millions

3. To search for a phrase with two or more words, you need to _____.

   a. underline the words   b. put the words in quotation marks

4. To find the information you need, you will probably need to look at _____.

   a. all of the pages   b. only the first two or three pages

5. The results of a web search are often referred to as _____.

   a. hits   b. keywords

A Read the scene from a TV program. Complete the tag questions.

I Didn't Do It!

Script from *Crime Suspect* Episode 6:
"Robbery on 12th Street"
Scene: Interview room in police station.

Detective 1: You robbed First National Bank,

_____*didn't you*_____?
                     1
You and Razor?

Danny: No! No, we didn't. I don't do bank

robberies.

Detective 1: Razor does. And you two are really

close friends.

Detective 2: You were at the bank yesterday afternoon, _____?
                                                                      2

Danny: I was opening an account. That's not a crime, _____?
                                                                 3

Detective 1: We can prove you both were involved, _____, Sam?
                                                             4

Detective 2: Yes, we sure can. Razor's fingerprints are all over the back door.

Danny: That doesn't mean I helped him, _____?
                                                  5

Detective 2: Then why did we find this key in your apartment? [*Shows Danny a key.*]

Danny: I've never seen it before.

Detective 1: It's a key to Razor's car, _____?
                                                   6

Danny: No. It's the key to . . .

B Look at A. Write short answers to the questions.

1. What do the detectives think Danny did? _robbed the First National Bank_

2. What does Danny say he was doing at the bank? _____

3. What did the detectives find on the back door? _____

4. What do you think? Did Danny help Razor rob the bank? Why?

_____

12 How Am I Doing?

A Complete the paragraphs. Use the words in the box.

~~overcome adversity~~	start a business	give back to the community
achieve her goal	had a dream	win a scholarship

David's life hadn't been easy, but his family helped him <u>overcome adversity</u> and get an education. When
1
he was a teenager, he _____. He
2
wanted to own a small restaurant. His father supported this dream and encouraged him to save money to

_____ in their community.
3

Goal: business owner

Yan-li always wanted to be a teacher. She needed money to go to college, so her only chance was to

_____. Everyone helped her to
4

_____. Now she's able to
5

_____ by helping children.
6

Goal: teacher

B Complete the sentences. Circle *a, b,* or *c.*

A person who…

1. is sure of himself is __c__.

   a. courageous   b. dedicated   c. confident

2. knows what is possible is ____.

   a. practical   b. confident   c. assertive

3. will try something a little scary is ____.

   a. competent   b. courageous   c. practical

4. works very hard is ____.

   a. dedicated   b. assertive   c. competent

A Read the prompt. Complete the essay. Use the sentences in the box.

Prompt: Describe one positive change in your life recently. How will this change affect your future?

> Fortunately, my family has been very helpful.
> Going back to school has been a positive change in my life.
> I will earn a good salary.
> ~~Last year, I decided to get a degree in hotel management at a local college.~~
> I am working during the day and studying at night.

P1   <u>Last year, I decided to get a degree in hotel management at a local college.</u>
1

It has been a positive change in my life.

P2   Now my life is very busy. _____
2

This means that I have less time for my family. _____
3

They know I have wanted to do this for a long time.

P3   Having more education will help me in the future. After I finish my degree,

I'll be able to get a great job. _____ That
4

will help me and my family.

P4   _____ Even though I am busy, it will
5

help me in the future. I know that someday I'll be a great hotel manager.

B Look at A. Answer the questions. Write *P1*, *P2 and P3*, or *P4*.

1. Which paragraph(s) make the writer's points, with supporting information and details?

   _____

2. Which paragraph(s) summarize the main points and gives a conclusion?

   _____

3. Which paragraph(s) introduces the topic of the essay?

   _____

A **Complete the sentences with the gerund form of the verb in parentheses.**

There are two college students who run the front desk at the Valley

Recreation Center. Karin knows a lot about ____using____ (use) the computer

1

to register new clients. She works very hard. Instead of _____ (leave)

                                             2

right at five o'clock every day, Karin stays late to plan activities. She cares

about _____ (help) people who have problems. Ricky, the other front

           3

desk clerk, is from Mexico. He's the soccer coach. He does a good job of

_____ (coach) the junior soccer team. He's wonderful with people, but

    4

he needs to work on _____ (speak) more clearly on the telephone.

                      5

B **Complete the sentences. Use the verbs in parentheses and gerunds.**

Hua-li (Holly) Xu works at a flower shop called City Flowers next to

the hospital. Holly ____works on creating____ (work on, create) beautiful

                       1

flower baskets. She likes her job because she _____

(believe in, make) the hospital patients feel better. Holly's boss, Leanne, also

                       2

_____ (care about, keep) the customers happy. Leanne is a

               3

good boss. She _____ (talk about, help) Holly open a small

                 4

flower shop of her own. Holly _____ (look forward to, start)

                     5

her own business.

C Complete the paragraph. Use the words in the box.

nervous about	responsible for	~~proud of~~	excited about

It was Luc's first day as an emergency technician. He felt very

_____proud of_____ being chosen out of ten applicants. Luc
         1

was _____ having this opportunity, but he was
         2

_____ making a mistake. His boss told Luc that he was
         3

_____ driving the ambulance safely. Luc tried his best
         4

to follow directions, and he did a good job on his first day.

D Complete the sentences with gerunds. Use your own ideas.

I'm interested in taking some courses in accounting.

1. I'm interested in _____.

2. I'm excited about _____.

3. I'm nervous about _____.

4. I'm tired of _____.

E Study the Grammar note. Then rewrite the sentences with gerunds.

> **Grammar note: Gerunds with *before, after, when***
>
> Gerunds are often used instead of time clauses with *before, after,* and *when*.
>
> **Time clause**   ***After I write*** *an essay, I ask a friend to read it.*
> **Gerund**   ***After writing*** *an essay, I ask a friend to read it.*

1. Before I begin an essay, I make notes about my ideas.

   Before beginning an essay, I make notes about my ideas.

2. When I write the essay, I don't worry about spelling.

   _____

3. After I finish the essay, I check for spelling mistakes.

   _____

4. After he reads my essay, Mr. Bloom usually gives me some good suggestions.

   _____

A **Number the sentences of the conversation in the correct order.**

_____ Yes, you forgot to tell them the patient's blood pressure.

_1_ Luc, you've done a great job today driving the ambulance.

_____ You need to be sure to give the doctors at the hospital the information they need.

_8_ Good idea. I will try to find one.

_____ I'll be sure to remember that. Anything else?

_____ Thanks. Is there anything I need to work on?

_____ Oh, I didn't realize there was a problem with the doctors.

_____ Yes, one more thing. I'd recommend taking an advanced training course.

B **Look at the conversation in A. Write a new ending.**

Luc: _Good idea. I will try to find one._

Supervisor: _Actually, there's one starting next week._

Luc: _____

Supervisor: _____

Luc: _____

Supervisor: _____

Luc: _____

C **Read the sentences. Then write polite requests or suggestions with gerunds. Use the words in parentheses.**

1. Can I recommend something? Take a training course. (I'd recommend)

   I'd recommend taking a training course.

2. Can I suggest something? Call ahead to the hospital. (I would suggest)

   _____

3. Please tell me where I should take this patient. (Would you mind)

   _____

4. Tell the doctors all of the patient's information. (May I suggest)

   _____

5. Can I recommend something? Listen closely to the patient. (I'd recommend)

   _____

A Read the article. Why is Leticia's story a positive example for others?

Leticia Walpole: A Success Story

Leticia Walpole was born in Mexico City. Her father did not believe that women should go to college, but with her mother's help, she secretly took college classes in mechanical engineering. At age 21, young Leticia purchased a bus ticket to Tijuana, Mexico, using her grandmother's gold necklace. In the Tijuana bus station, studying a newspaper, she found an ad for a job as a housekeeper.

After working as a housekeeper for a year, and with the help of her employer, Leticia was hired as a supervisor at an American toy company in Mexico. The company president was so impressed with her management skills that he helped her move to Los Angeles. Arriving in Los Angeles, she was alone and had only $100 and a suitcase of clothes. She needed a job, and she also had to learn English.

Within a week, with the help of an American family, Leticia was taking

Leticia Walpole helps out at a recent community event.

English classes at a community college and working three jobs. Soon she applied for a job with the National Guard.[1] They offered her more training in engineering. Later, when the Guard said that its officers had to have a college degree, she returned to college. She earned bachelor's degrees in science, Spanish, and liberal arts.

Now Leticia Walpole gives talks in many organizations and schools in the Hispanic community. She is an example to young people from other countries of someone who overcame obstacles and achieved their dreams.

[1]National Guard: an organization that supports the U.S. military.

B Look at A. Mark the sentences *T* (true) or *F* (false).

_F_ 1. Leticia Walpole's father believed women should go to college.

____ 2. Leticia found her first job by reading a newspaper.

____ 3. The American toy company was in Los Angeles.

____ 4. Leticia knew how to speak English when she arrived in the U.S.

____ 5. Leticia got a bachelor's degree in management.

____ 6. Now Leticia uses her experience as an example to help others.

A Holly Xu has just taken a leadership test. How many points does she have? Add them up. Is she a good leader?

TAKE A TEST TO FIND OUT:

Are You a **Leader?**

	Often (3 pts)	Sometimes (2 pts)	Never (1 pt)
1 I win awards or scholarships for success at school or the workplace.	☐	☒	☐
2 When I have difficulty with a task, I ask for suggestions for <u>improving</u> my work.	☒	☐	☐
3 If a co-worker has difficulty in completing a job, I try to get someone to help.	☒	☐	☐
4 I'm comfortable when speaking in front of other people.	☐	☒	☐
5 I'm very good at reading maps.	☒	☐	☐
6 I enjoy helping others learn new skills.	☒	☐	☐
7 I'm happier working with others than alone.	☐	☐	☒
8 I dream about being famous one day.	☐	☐	☒
9 I'm on time for meetings.	☒	☐	☐
10 I don't mind going to a restaurant or a movie alone.	☐	☒	☐

TOTAL EACH COLUMN: <u>15</u> ___ ___

TOTAL POINTS: ___

27–30 points	18–26 points	Fewer than 18 points
You are a natural leader. Other people look to you for leadership.	You can be a leader at times. But other times you're happy to follow others.	We can't all be leaders. People who are good followers are very important, too!

B Look at A. Complete the tasks.

1. In item 2, a gerund is underlined. There are seven more gerunds in the test. Find them and underline them.

2. Complete the test for yourself. Are you a leader?

UNIT 1

Look at the graph. Do the math. Answer the question.

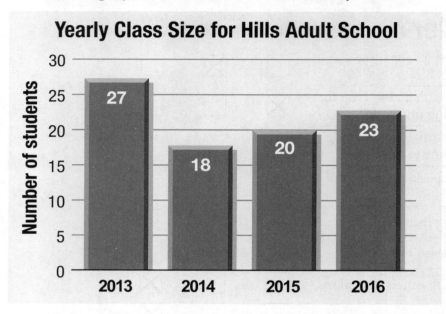

Yearly Class Size for Hills Adult School

What was the average* number of students per class at Hills Adult School for the four-year period from 2013 to 2016? _____

*average = total number of students for 4 years, divided by 4

UNIT 2

Read the story. Do the math. Answer the question.

> Before the hurricane hit, 100,000 Floridians left their homes. Luckily, when the hurricane hit, very few homes were damaged. On Thursday, 75,000 people returned to their homes; another 24,500 were allowed to return on Friday. However, some homes are still without electricity or water. Local officials expect the rest of the people to return home tomorrow.

On the day the story was written, how many people were still out of their homes?

_____

A Read the information in the chart. Do the math. Complete the time column.
Then answer the question.

Route	Distance (miles)	Speed limit	Time* (minutes)
1. Airport Drive to Clark Ave	15	40 mph	_____
2. Highway 24 to Clark Ave	17	60 mph	_____

(Hint: To calculate time, divide the distance by the miles per hour. Then multiply by 60.)

If there's no traffic, how much time can you save on Highway 24? _____

B Read the confirmation email for a hotel reservation. Do the math. Answer
the questions.

1. How many nights is Billy planning to stay at the Motel 22?

   _____

2. How much is Billy's room per night (room rate plus taxes and charges)?

   _____

3. What will be the total cost of his stay at Motel 22?

   _____

Read the extract from Hanna's resume. Do the math. Answer the questions.

Employment history

6/1/15 – present	Home health-care aide, Sunnyside Associates, Austin
11/1/13 – 5/31/15	Cashier, Tannelo Department Stores, Austin
9/1/09 – 4/28/13	File Clerk, Central Market Supplies, Austin
9/1/07 – 7/31/09	Receptionist, One World Daycare Center, Austin

1. How long had Hanna been a cashier before she became a home health-care aide?

   _____

2. How long did she work as a file clerk?

   _____

3. How long did she work at a daycare center?

   _____

UNIT 5

Read the chart about workplace safety. Then look at the groups of jobs below. Do the math. Which group has more illnesses and injuries?

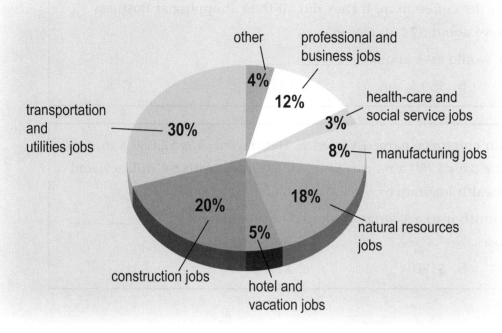

PERCENT OF WORKPLACE INJURIES BY JOB TYPE, 2014

other 4%

professional and business jobs 12%

health-care and social service jobs 3%

manufacturing jobs 8%

natural resources jobs 18%

hotel and vacation jobs 5%

construction jobs 20%

transportation and utilities jobs 30%

Source: *www.bls.gov*

Group 1: manufacturing jobs, construction jobs, natural resources jobs

Group 2: professional and business jobs, hotel and vacation jobs, transportation and utilities jobs

UNIT 6

Read the problem. Do the math. Answer the question.

Martinez Electronics			Name: Tom Tran		Check # 3133
Gross Pay	Social Security	Medicare	Federal Tax	State Tax	**Net Pay**
$421.40	$26.13	$6.11	$11.03	$13.80	**$355.36**

Tom called Ms. Bell in Payroll because he thinks there is an error on his paycheck. He thinks his net pay is incorrect. What should Tom's net pay be? _____

UNIT 7

Read the stories. Do the math. Circle a, b, or c.

1. Jon and Yen now spend about $150.00 a week on supplies like napkins, paper towels, and cups for the coffee shop. If they did all their shopping at Business Mart, they would save about $22.50 a week.

   In four weeks, they would save about _____.

   a. $150   b. $50   c. $90

2. Jon and Yen have an employee named Veronica. Her paycheck is $2,050 a month after deductions. She pays $750 a month for rent, $125 a month for utilities, and $180 a month for health insurance.

   If she put $120 a month into a savings account, she would have _____ left for other expenses.

   a. $875   b. $120   c. $1,175

UNIT 8

Read the story. Do the math. Answer the questions.

Sylvia wants to order two toys for her grandchildren from a catalog. One toy costs $11.95, and the other toy costs $16.95, including tax. The company charges 10% shipping and handling on orders under $50. On orders over $50, shipping and handling is free.

1. How much will Sylvia's order be, including shipping and handling?

   _____

2. Sylvia doesn't want to pay shipping. How much more does she need to spend to get free shipping?

   _____

UNIT 9

Read about Teresa. Do the math. Circle the answer.

When Teresa walks, she uses a pedometer, a small device that counts the steps she takes. She takes about 38 steps per 100 feet. There are 5,280 feet in one mile. About how many steps does she take in a mile?

a. 1,600   b. 2,000   c. 2,800

UNIT 10

A **Read the story. Do the math. Answer the question.**

There were 51 people present at the Alto Plano city council meeting. Thirty-two people voted in favor of adding a recycling center to South Street Park. They needed a 2/3 majority to win. Did the recycling center pass?

_____

B **Study the pie chart of Alto Plano's annual budget. Do the math and answer the questions.**

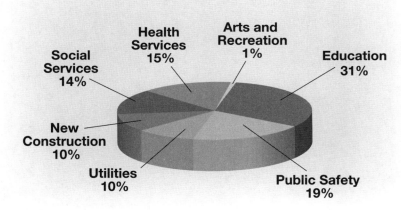

Alto Plano Annual Budget

1. Which two programs together use half of the city's budget?

   _____

2. If the total city budget is one hundred million dollars, how much is the city spending on arts and recreation in a year?

   _____

UNIT 11

Look at the website counter. Do the math. Answer the question.

Visitors today: 6 2 5 ☐ ☐ ☐
Visitors last year: 1 4 9 6 5 0

Today was an unusual day for ApartmentSearch.apt. The website gets about the same number of visitors, or hits, every day. Today was a very busy day. How many more hits did the site get today than it usually gets in a day? _____

(Hint: There are 365 days in a year.)

UNIT 12

Read about Luc. Do the math. Answer the question.

Luc is certified as a basic EMT (Emergency Medical Technician). To become an intermediate EMT, he needs about 200 more hours of training. If he takes a class that meets every Saturday for 4 hours, how long will it take him to be certified at the intermediate level?

_____ weeks